THE PELICAN SHAKESPEARE
GENERAL EDITORS

STEPHEN ORGEL
A. R. BRAUNMULLER

The Taming of the Shrew

An eighteenth-century Petruchio, the comedian Harry
Woodward (1717–1777), in Garrick's popular adaptation
Catherine and Petruchio. From Bell's Shakespeare, 1775.

William Shakespeare

—

The Taming of the Shrew

EDITED BY STEPHEN ORGEL

PENGUIN BOOKS

PENGUIN BOOKS

Published by the Penguin Group

Penguin Group (USA) Inc., 375 Hudson Street, New York, New York 10014, U.S.A.

Penguin Group (Canada), 90 Eglinton Avenue East, Suite 700, Toronto, Ontario,
Canada M4P 2Y3 (a division of Pearson Penguin Canada Inc.)

Penguin Books Ltd, 80 Strand, London WC2R 0RL, England

Penguin Ireland, 25 St Stephen's Green, Dublin 2, Ireland
(a division of Penguin Books Ltd)

Penguin Group (Australia), 250 Camberwell Road, Camberwell, Victoria 3124,
Australia (a division of Pearson Australia Group Pty Ltd)

Penguin Books India Pvt Ltd, 11 Community Centre, Panchsheel Park,
New Delhi – 110 017, India

Penguin Group (NZ), 67 Apollo Drive, Rosedale, North Shore,
Auckland 0745, New Zealand (a division of Pearson New Zealand Ltd)

Penguin Books (South Africa) (Pty) Ltd, 24 Sturdee Avenue, Rosebank, Johannesburg 2196, South Africa

Penguin Books Ltd, Registered Offices: 80 Strand, London WC2R 0RL, England

The Taming of the Shrew edited by Richard Hosley published in the
United States of America in Penguin Books 1964
Revised edition published 1970
This new edition edited by Stephen Orgel published 2000

20 19 18 17 16 15 14 13 12

Copyright © Penguin Books Inc., 1964, 1970
Copyright © Penguin Putnam Inc., 2000
All rights reserved

ISBN 978-0-14-071451-7
(CIP data available)

Printed in the United States of America
Set in Adobe Garamond
Designed by Virginia Norey

Contents

Publisher's Note

IT IS ALMOST half a century since the first volumes of the Pelican Shakespeare appeared under the general editorship of Alfred Harbage. The fact that a new edition, rather than simply a revision, has been undertaken reflects the profound changes textual and critical studies of Shakespeare have undergone in the past twenty years. For the new Pelican series, the texts of the plays and poems have been thoroughly revised in accordance with recent scholarship, and in some cases have been entirely reedited. New introductions and notes have been provided in all the volumes. But the new Shakespeare is also designed as a successor to the original series; the previous editions have been taken into account, and the advice of the previous editors has been solicited where it was feasible to do so.

Certain textual features of the new Pelican Shakespeare should be particularly noted. All lines are numbered that contain a word, phrase, or allusion explained in the glossarial notes. In addition, for convenience, every tenth line is also numbered, in italics when no annotation is indicated. The intrusive and often inaccurate place headings inserted by early editors are omitted (as is becoming standard practice), but for the convenience of those who miss them, an indication of locale now appears as the first item in the annotation of each scene.

In the interest of both elegance and utility, each speech prefix is set in a separate line when the speaker's lines are in verse, except when those words form the second half of a verse line. Thus the verse form of the speech is kept visually intact. What is printed as verse and what is printed as prose has, in general, the authority of the original texts. Departures from the original texts in this regard have only the authority of editorial tradition and the judgment of the Pelican editors; and, in a few instances, are admittedly arbitrary.

The Theatrical World

ECONOMIC REALITIES determined the theatrical world in which Shakespeare's plays were written, performed, and received. For centuries in England, the primary theatrical tradition was nonprofessional. Craft guilds (or "mysteries") provided religious drama – mystery plays – as part of the celebration of religious and civic festivals, and schools and universities staged classical and neoclassical drama in both Latin and English as part of their curricula. In these forms, drama was established and socially acceptable. Professional theater, in contrast, existed on the margins of society. The acting companies were itinerant; playhouses could be any available space – the great halls of the aristocracy, town squares, civic halls, inn yards, fair booths, or open fields – and income was sporadic, dependent on the passing of the hat or on the bounty of local patrons. The actors, moreover, were considered little better than vagabonds, constantly in danger of arrest or expulsion.

In the late 1560s and 1570s, however, English professional theater began to gain respectability. Wealthy aristocrats fond of drama – the Lord Admiral, for example, or the Lord Chamberlain – took acting companies under their protection so that the players technically became members of their households and were no longer subject to arrest as homeless or masterless men. Permanent theaters were first built at this time as well, allowing the companies to control and charge for entry to their performances.

Shakespeare's livelihood, and the stunning artistic explosion in which he participated, depended on pragmatic and architectural effort. Professional theater requires ways to restrict access to its offerings; if it does not, and admission fees cannot be charged, the actors do not get paid, the costumes go to a pawnbroker, and there is no such thing as a professional, ongoing theatrical tradition. The answer to that economic need arrived in the late 1560s and 1570s with the creation of the so-called public or amphitheater playhouse. Recent discoveries indicate that the precursor of the Globe playhouse in London (where Shakespeare's mature plays were presented) and the Rose theater (which presented Christopher Marlowe's plays and some of Shakespeare's earliest ones) was the Red Lion theater of 1567. Archaeological studies of the foundations of the Rose and Globe theaters have revealed that the open-air theater of the 1590s and later was probably a polygonal building with fourteen to twenty or twenty-four sides, multistoried, from 75 to 100 feet in diameter, with a raised, partly covered "thrust" stage that projected into a group of standing patrons, or "groundlings," and a covered gallery, seating up to 2,500 or more (very crowded) spectators.

These theaters might have been about half full on any given day, though the audiences were larger on holidays or when a play was advertised, as old and new were, through printed playbills posted around London. The metropolitan area's late-Tudor, early-Stuart population (circa 1590-1620) has been estimated at about 150,000 to 250,000. It has been supposed that in the mid-1590s there were about 15,000 spectators per week at the public theaters; thus, as many as 10 percent of the local population went to the theater regularly. Consequently, the theaters' repertories – the plays available for this experienced and frequent audience – had to change often: in the month between September 15 and October 15, 1595, for instance, the Lord Admiral's Men performed twenty-eight times in eighteen different plays.

Since natural light illuminated the amphitheaters' stages, performances began between noon and two o'clock and ran without a break for two or three hours. They often concluded with a jig, a fencing display, or some other nondramatic exhibition. Weather conditions determined the season for the amphitheaters: plays were performed every day (including Sundays, sometimes, to clerical dismay) except during Lent – the forty days before Easter – or periods of plague, or sometimes during the summer months when law courts were not in session and the most affluent members of the audience were not in London.

To a modern theatergoer, an amphitheater stage like that of the Rose or Globe would appear an unfamiliar mixture of plainness and elaborate decoration. Much of the structure was carved or painted, sometimes to imitate marble; elsewhere, as under the canopy projecting over the stage, to represent the stars and the zodiac. Appropriate painted canvas pictures (of Jerusalem, for example, if the play was set in that city) were apparently hung on the wall behind the acting area, and tragedies were accompanied by black hangings, presumably something like crepe festoons or bunting. Although these theaters did not employ what we would call scenery, early modern spectators saw numerous large props, such as the "bar" at which a prisoner stood during a trial, the "mossy bank" where lovers reclined, an arbor for amorous conversation, a chariot, gallows, tables, trees, beds, thrones, writing desks, and so forth. Audiences might learn a scene's location from a sign (reading "Athens," for example) carried across the stage (as in Bertolt Brecht's twentieth-century productions). Equally captivating (and equally irritating to the theater's enemies) were the rich costumes and personal props the actors used: the most valuable items in the surviving theatrical inventories are the swords, gowns, robes, crowns, and other items worn or carried by the performers.

Magic appealed to Shakespeare's audiences as much as it does to us today, and the theater exploited many deceptive and spectacular devices. A winch in the loft above the stage, called "the heavens," could lower and raise actors playing gods, goddesses, and other supernatural figures to and from the main acting area, just as one or more trapdoors permitted entrances and exits to and from the area, called "hell," beneath the stage. Actors wore elementary makeup such as wigs, false beards, and face paint, and they employed pig's bladders filled with animal blood to make wounds seem more real. They had rudimentary but effective ways of pretending to behead or hang a person. Supernumeraries (stagehands or actors not needed in a particular scene) could make thunder sounds (by shaking a metal sheet or rolling an iron ball down a chute) and show lightning (by blowing inflammable resin through tubes into a flame). Elaborate fireworks enhanced the effects of dragons flying through the air or imitated such celestial phenomena as comets, shooting stars, and multiple suns. Horses' hoofbeats, bells (located perhaps in the tower above the stage), trumpets and drums, clocks, cannon shots and gunshots, and the like were common sound effects. And the music of viols, cornets, oboes, and recorders was a regular feature of theatrical performances.

For two relatively brief spans, from the late 1570s to 1590 and from 1599 to 1614, the amphitheaters competed with the so-called private, or indoor, theaters, which originated as, or later represented themselves as, educational institutions training boys as singers for church services and court performances. These indoor theaters had two features that were distinct from the amphitheaters': their personnel and their playing spaces. The amphitheaters' adult companies included both adult men, who played the male roles, and boys, who played the female roles; the private, or indoor, theater companies, on the other hand, were entirely composed of boys aged about 8 to 16, who were, or could pretend to be, candidates for singers in a church or a royal boys' choir. (Until 1660, professional theatrical companies included no women.) The playing space would appear much more familiar to modern audiences than the long-vanished amphitheaters; the later indoor theaters were, in fact, the ancestors of the typical modern theater. They were enclosed spaces, usually rectangular, with the stage filling one end of the rectangle and the audience arrayed in seats or benches across (and sometimes lining) the building's longer axis. These spaces staged plays less frequently than the public theaters (perhaps only once a week) and held far fewer spectators than the amphitheaters: about 200 to 600, as opposed to 2,500 or more. Fewer patrons mean a smaller gross income, unless each pays more. Not surprisingly, then, private theaters charged higher prices than the amphitheaters, probably sixpence, as opposed to a penny for the cheapest entry.

Protected from the weather, the indoor theaters presented plays later in the day than the amphitheaters, and used artificial illumination – candles in sconces or candelabra. But candles melt, and need replacing, snuffing, and trimming, and these practical requirements may have been part of the reason the indoor theaters introduced breaks in the performance, the intermission so dear to the heart of theatergoers and to the pocketbooks of theater concessionaires ever since. Whether motivated by the need to tend to the candles or by the entrepreneurs' wishing to sell oranges and liquor, or both, the indoor theaters eventually established the modern convention of the non-continuous performance. In the early modern "private" theater, musical performances apparently filled the intermissions, which in Stuart theater jargon seem to have been called "acts."

At the end of the first decade of the seventeenth century, the distinction between public amphitheaters and private indoor companies ceased. For various cultural, political, and economic reasons, individual companies gained control of both the public, open-air theaters and the indoor ones, and companies mixing adult men and boys took over the formerly "private" theaters. Despite the death of the boys' companies and of their highly innovative theaters (for which such luminous playwrights as Ben Jonson, George Chapman, and John Marston wrote), their playing spaces and conventions had an immense impact on subsequent plays: not merely for the intervals (which stressed the artistic and architectonic importance of "acts"), but also because they introduced political and social satire as a popular dramatic ingredient, even in tragedy, and a wider range of actorly effects, encouraged by their more intimate playing spaces.

Even the briefest sketch of the Shakespearean theatrical world would be incomplete without some comment on the social and cultural dimensions of theaters and playing in the period. In an intensely hierarchical and status-conscious society, professional actors and their ventures had hardly any respectability; as we have indicated, to protect themselves against laws designed to curb vagabondage and the increase of masterless men, actors resorted to the near-fiction that they were the servants of noble masters, and wore their distinctive livery. Hence the company for which Shakespeare wrote in the 1590s called itself the Lord Chamberlain's Men and pretended that the public, money-getting performances were in fact rehearsals for private performances before that high court official. From 1598, the Privy Council had licensed theatrical companies, and after 1603, with the accession of King James I, the companies gained explicit royal protection, just as the Queen's Men had for a time under Queen Elizabeth. The Chamberlain's Men became the King's Men, and the other companies were patronized by the other members of the royal family.

These designations were legal fictions that half-concealed an important economic and social development, the evolution away from the theater's organization on the model of the guild, a self-regulating confraternity of individual artisans, into a proto-capitalist organization. Shakespeare's company became a joint-stock company, where persons who supplied capital and, in some cases,

such as Shakespeare's, capital and talent, employed themselves and others in earning a return on that capital. This
development meant that actors and theater companies
were outside both the traditional guild structures, which
required some form of civic or royal charter, and the feu-
dal household organization of master-and-servant. This
anomalous, maverick social and economic condition
made theater companies practically unruly and poten-
tially even dangerous; consequently, numerous official
bodies – including the London metropolitan and ecclesi-
astical authorities as well as, occasionally, the royal court
itself – tried, without much success, to control and even
to disband them.

Public officials had good reason to want to close the
theaters: they were attractive nuisances – they drew often
riotous crowds, they were always noisy, and they could be
politically offensive and socially insubordinate. Until the
Civil War, however, anti-theatrical forces failed to shut
down professional theater, for many reasons – limited
surveillance and few police powers, tensions or outright
hostilities among the agencies that sought to check or
channel theatrical activity, and lack of clear policies for
control. Another reason must have been the theaters' un-
deniable popularity. Curtailing any activity enjoyed by
such a substantial percentage of the population was difficult, as various Roman emperors attempting to limit cir-
cuses had learned, and the Tudor-Stuart audience was not
merely large, it was socially diverse and included women.
The prevalence of public entertainment in this period
has been underestimated. In fact, fairs, holidays, games,
sporting events, the equivalent of modern parades, freak
shows, and street exhibitions all abounded, but the theater was the most widely and frequently available entertainment to which people of every class had access. That
fact helps account both for its quantity and for the fear
and anger it aroused.

William Shakespeare of
Stratford-upon-Avon, Gentleman

Many people have said that we know very little about William Shakespeare's life – pinheads and postcards are often mentioned as appropriately tiny surfaces on which to record the available information. More imaginatively and perhaps more correctly, Ralph Waldo Emerson wrote, "Shakespeare is the only biographer of Shakespeare. . . . So far from Shakespeare's being the least known, he is the one person in all modern history fully known to us."

In fact, we know more about Shakespeare's life than we do about almost any other English writer's of his era. His last will and testament (dated March 25, 1616) survives, as do numerous legal contracts and court documents involving Shakespeare as principal or witness, and parish records in Stratford and London. Shakespeare appears quite often in official records of King James's royal court, and of course Shakespeare's name appears on numerous title pages and in the written and recorded words of his literary contemporaries Robert Greene, Henry Chettle, Francis Meres, John Davies of Hereford, Ben Jonson, and many others. Indeed, if we make due allowance for the bloating of modern, run-of-the-mill bureaucratic records, more information has survived over the past four hundred years about William Shakespeare of Stratford-upon-Avon, Warwickshire, than is likely to survive in the next four hundred years about any reader of these words.

What we do not have are entire categories of information – Shakespeare's private letters or diaries, drafts and revisions of poems and plays, critical prefaces or essays, commendatory verse for other writers' works, or instructions guiding his fellow actors in their performances, for instance – that we imagine would help us understand and appreciate his surviving writings. For all we know, many such data never existed as written records. Many literary and theatrical critics, not knowing what might once have existed, more or less cheerfully accept the situation; some even make a theoretical virtue of it by claiming that such data are irrelevant to understanding and interpreting the plays and poems.

So, what do we know about William Shakespeare, the man responsible for thirty-seven or perhaps more plays, more than 150 sonnets, two lengthy narrative poems, and some shorter poems?

While many families by the name of Shakespeare (or some variant spelling) can be identified in the English Midlands as far back as the twelfth century, it seems likely that the dramatist's grandfather, Richard, moved to Snitterfield, a town not far from Stratford-upon-Avon, sometime before 1529. In Snitterfield, Richard Shakespeare leased farmland from the very wealthy Robert Arden. By 1552, Richard's son John had moved to a large house on Henley Street in Stratford-upon-Avon, the house that stands today as "The Birthplace." In Stratford, John Shakespeare traded as a glover, dealt in wool, and lent money at interest; he also served in a variety of civic posts, including "High Bailiff," the municipality's equivalent of mayor. In 1557, he married Robert Arden's youngest daughter, Mary. Mary and John had four sons – William was the oldest – and four daughters, of whom only Joan outlived her most celebrated sibling. William was baptized (an event entered in the Stratford parish church records) on April 26, 1564, and it has become customary, without any good factual support, to suppose he was born on April 23, which happens to be the feast day of Saint George, patron saint of England, and is also the date on which he died, in 1616. Shakespeare married Anne Hathaway in 1582, when he was eighteen and she was twenty-six; their first child was born five months later. It has been generally assumed that the marriage was enforced and subsequently unhappy, but these are only assumptions; it has been estimated, for instance, that up to one third of Elizabethan brides were pregnant when they married. Anne and William Shakespeare had three children: Susanna, who married a prominent local physician, John Hall; and the twins Hamnet, who died young in 1596, and Judith, who married Thomas Quiney – apparently a rather shady individual. The name Hamnet was unusual but not unique: he and his twin sister were named for their godparents, Shakespeare's neighbors Hamnet and Judith Sadler. Shakespeare's father died in 1601 (the year of *Hamlet*), and Mary Arden Shakespeare died in 1608 (the year of *Coriolanus*). William Shakespeare's last surviving direct descendant was his granddaughter Elizabeth Hall, who died in 1670.

Between the birth of the twins in 1585 and a clear reference to Shakespeare as a practicing London dramatist in Robert Greene's sensationalizing, satiric pamphlet, *Greene's Groatsworth of Wit* (1592), there is no record of where William Shakespeare was or what he was doing. These seven so-called lost years have been imaginatively filled by scholars and other students of Shakespeare: some think he traveled to Italy, or fought in the Low Countries, or studied law or medicine, or worked as an apprentice actor/writer, and so on to even more fanciful possibilities. Whatever the biographical facts for those "lost" years, Greene's nasty remarks in 1592 testify to professional envy and to the fact that Shakespeare already had a successful career in London. Speaking to his fellow playwrights, Greene warns both generally and specifically:

> . . . trust them [actors] not: for there is an upstart crow, beautified with our feathers, that with his tiger's heart wrapped in a player's hide supposes he is as well able to bombast out a blank verse as the best of you; and being an absolute Johannes Factotum, is in his own conceit the only Shake-scene in a country.

The passage mimics a line from *3 Henry VI* (hence the play must have been performed before Greene wrote) and seems to say that "Shake-scene" is both actor and playwright, a jack-of-all-trades. That same year, Henry Chettle protested Greene's remarks in *Kind-Heart's Dream,* and each of the next two years saw the publication of poems – *Venus and Adonis* and *The Rape of Lucrece,* respectively – publicly ascribed to (and dedicated by) Shakespeare. Early in 1595 he was named one of the senior members of a prominent acting company, the Lord Chamberlain's Men, when they received payment for court performances during the 1594 Christmas season.

Clearly, Shakespeare had achieved both success and reputation in London. In 1596, upon Shakespeare's application, the College of Arms granted his father the now-familiar coat of arms he had taken the first steps to obtain almost twenty years before, and in 1598, John's son – now permitted to call himself "gentleman" – took a 10 percent share in the new Globe playhouse. In 1597, he bought a substantial bourgeois house, called New Place, in Stratford – the garden remains, but Shakespeare's house, several times rebuilt, was torn down in 1759 – and over the next few years Shakespeare spent large sums buying land and making other investments in the town and its environs. Though he worked in London, his family remained in Stratford, and he seems always to have considered Stratford the home he would eventually return to. Something approaching a disinterested appreciation of Shakespeare's popular and professional status appears in Francis Meres's *Palladis Tamia* (1598), a not especially imaginative and perhaps therefore persuasive record of literary reputations. Reviewing contemporary English writers, Meres lists the titles of many of Shakespeare's plays, including one not now known, *Love's Labor's Won,* and praises his "mellifluous & hony-tongued" "sugred Sonnets," which were then circulating in manuscript (they were first collected in 1609). Meres describes Shakespeare as "one of the best" English playwrights of both comedy and tragedy. In *Remains . . . Concerning Britain* (1605),

William Camden – a more authoritative source than the imitative Meres – calls Shakespeare one of the "most pregnant witts of these our times" and joins him with such writers as Chapman, Daniel, Jonson, Marston, and Spenser. During the first decades of the seventeenth century, publishers began to attribute numerous play quartos, including some non-Shakespearean ones, to Shakespeare, either by name or initials, and we may assume that they deemed Shakespeare's name and supposed authorship, true or false, commercially attractive.

For the next ten years or so, various records show Shakespeare's dual career as playwright and man of the theater in London, and as an important local figure in Stratford. In 1608-9 his acting company – designated the "King's Men" soon after King James had succeeded Queen Elizabeth in 1603 – rented, refurbished, and opened a small interior playing space, the Blackfriars theater, in London, and Shakespeare was once again listed as a substantial sharer in the group of proprietors of the playhouse. By May 11, 1612, however, he describes himself as a Stratford resident in a London lawsuit – an indication that he had withdrawn from day-to-day professional activity and returned to the town where he had always had his main financial interests. When Shakespeare bought a substantial residential building in London, the Blackfriars Gatehouse, close to the theater of the same name, on March 10, 1613, he is recorded as William Shakespeare "of Stratford upon Avon in the county of Warwick, gentleman," and he named several London residents as the building's trustees. Still, he continued to participate in theatrical activity: when the new Earl of Rutland needed an allegorical design to bear as a shield, or *impresa,* at the celebration of King James's Accession Day, March 24, 1613, the earl's accountant recorded a payment of 44 shillings to Shakespeare for the device with its motto.

For the last few years of his life, Shakespeare evidently

concentrated his activities in the town of his birth. Most of the final records concern business transactions in Stratford, ending with the notation of his death on April 23, 1616, and burial in Holy Trinity Church, Stratford-upon-Avon.

THE QUESTION OF AUTHORSHIP

The history of ascribing Shakespeare's plays (the poems do not come up so often) to someone else began, as it continues, peculiarly. The earliest published claim that someone else wrote Shakespeare's plays appeared in an 1856 article by Delia Bacon in the American journal *Putnam's Monthly* – although an Englishman, Thomas Wilmot, had shared his doubts in private (even secretive) conversations with friends near the end of the eighteenth century. Bacon's was a sad personal history that ended in madness and poverty, but the year after her article, she published, with great difficulty and the bemused assistance of Nathaniel Hawthorne (then United States Consul in Liverpool, England), her *Philosophy of the Plays of Shakspere Unfolded.* This huge, ornately written, confusing farrago is almost unreadable; sometimes its intents, to say nothing of its arguments, disappear entirely beneath near-raving, ecstatic writing. Tumbled in with much supposed "philosophy" appear the claims that Francis Bacon (from whom Delia Bacon eventually claimed descent), Walter Ralegh, and several other contemporaries of Shakespeare's had written the plays. The book had little impact except as a ridiculed curiosity.

Once proposed, however, the issue gained momentum among people whose conviction was the greater in proportion to their ignorance of sixteenth- and seventeenth-century English literature, history, and society. Another American amateur, Catherine P. Ashmead Windle, made the next influential contribution to the cause when she published *Report to the British Museum* (1882), wherein she promised to open "the Cipher of Francis Bacon," though what she mostly offers, in the words of S. Schoenbaum, is "demented allegorizing." An entire new cottage industry grew from Windle's suggestion that the texts contain hidden, cryptographically discoverable ciphers – "clues" – to their authorship; and today there are not only books devoted to the putative ciphers, but also pamphlets, journals, and newsletters.

Although Baconians have led the pack of those seeking a substitute Shakespeare, in *"Shakespeare" Identified* (1920), J. Thomas Looney became the first published "Oxfordian" when he proposed Edward de Vere, seventeenth earl of Oxford, as the secret author of Shakespeare's plays. Also for Oxford and his "authorship" there are today dedicated societies, articles, journals, and books. Less popular candidates – Queen Elizabeth and Christopher Marlowe among them – have had adherents, but the movement seems to have divided into two main contending factions, Baconian and Oxfordian. (For further details on all the candidates for "Shakespeare," see S. Schoenbaum, *Shakespeare's Lives,* 2nd ed., 1991.)

The Baconians, the Oxfordians, and supporters of other candidates have one trait in common – they are snobs. Every pro-Bacon or pro-Oxford tract sooner or later claims that the historical William Shakespeare of Stratford-upon-Avon could not have written the plays because he could not have had the training, the university education, the experience, and indeed the imagination or background their author supposedly possessed. Only a learned genius like Bacon or an aristocrat like Oxford could have written such fine plays. (As it happens, lucky male children of the middle class had access to better education than most aristocrats in Elizabethan England – and Oxford was not particularly well educated.) Shakespeare received in the Stratford grammar school a formal education that would daunt many college graduates today; and popular rival playwrights such as the very learned Ben Jonson and George Chapman, both of whom also lacked university training, achieved great artistic success, without being taken as Bacon or Oxford.

Besides snobbery, one other quality characterizes the authorship controversy: lack of evidence. A great deal of testimony from Shakespeare's time shows that Shakespeare wrote Shakespeare's plays and that his contemporaries recognized them as distinctive and distinctly superior. (Some of that contemporary evidence is collected in E. K. Chambers, *William Shakespeare: A Study of Facts and Problems,* 2 vols., 1930.) Since that testimony comes from Shakespeare's enemies and theatrical competitors as well as from his co-workers and from the Elizabethan equivalent of literary journalists, it seems unlikely that, if any of these sources had known he was a fraud, they would have failed to record that fact.

Books About Shakespeare's Theater

Useful scholarly studies of theatrical life in Shakespeare's day include: G. E. Bentley, *The Jacobean and Caroline Stage,* 7 vols. (1941–68), and the same author's *The Professions of Dramatist and Player in Shakespeare's Time, 1590–1642* (1986); E. K. Chambers, *The Elizabethan Stage,* 4 vols. (1923); R. A. Foakes, *Illustrations of the English Stage, 1580–1642* (1985); Andrew Gurr, *The Shakespearean Stage,* 3rd ed. (1992), and the same author's *Play-going in Shakespeare's London,* 2nd ed. (1996); Edwin Nungezer, *A Dictionary of Actors* (1929); Carol Chillington Rutter, ed., *Documents of the Rose Playhouse* (1984).

Books About Shakespeare's Life

The following books provide scholarly, documented accounts of Shakespeare's life: G. E. Bentley, *Shakespeare: A Biographical Handbook* (1961); E. K. Chambers, *William Shakespeare: A Study of Facts and Problems,* 2 vols. (1930); S. Schoenbaum, *William Shakespeare: A Compact*

Documentary Life (1977); and *Shakespeare's Lives,* 2nd ed. (1991), by the same author. Many scholarly editions of Shakespeare's complete works print brief compilations of essential dates and events. References to Shakespeare's works up to 1700 are collected in C. M. Ingleby et al., *The Shakespeare Allusion-Book,* rev. ed., 2 vols. (1932).

The Texts of Shakespeare

As far as we know, only one manuscript conceivably in Shakespeare's own hand may (and even this is much disputed) exist: a few pages of a play called *Sir Thomas More,* which apparently was never performed. What we do have, as later readers, performers, scholars, students, are printed texts. The earliest of these survive in two forms: quartos and folios. Quartos (from the Latin for "four") are small books, printed on sheets of paper that were then folded in fours, to make eight double-sided pages. When these were bound together, the result was a squarish, eminently portable volume that sold for the relatively small sum of sixpence (translating in modern terms to about $5.00). In folios, on the other hand, the sheets are folded only once, in half, producing large, impressive volumes taller than they are wide. This was the format for important works of philosophy, science, theology, and literature (the major precedent for a folio Shakespeare was Ben Jonson's *Works,* 1616). The decision to print the works of a popular playwright in folio is an indication of how far up on the social scale the theatrical profession had come during Shakespeare's lifetime. The Shakespeare folio was an expensive book, selling for between fifteen and eighteen shillings, depending on the binding (in modern terms, from about $150 to $180). Twenty Shakespeare plays of the thirty-seven that survive first appeared in quarto, seventeen of which appeared during Shakespeare's lifetime; the rest of the plays are found only in folio.

The First Folio was published in 1623, seven years after Shakespeare's death, and was authorized by his fellow actors, the co-owners of the King's Men. This publication was certainly a mark of the company's enormous respect for Shakespeare; but it was also a way of turning the old plays, most of which were no longer current in the playhouse, into ready money (the folio includes only Shakespeare's plays, not his sonnets or other nondramatic verse). Whatever the motives behind the publication of the folio, the texts it preserves constitute the basis for almost all later editions of the playwright's works. The texts, however, differ from those of the earlier quartos, sometimes in minor respects but often significantly – most strikingly in the two texts of *King Lear,* but also in important ways in *Hamlet, Othello,* and *Troilus and Cressida.* (The variants are recorded in the textual notes to each play in the new Pelican series.) The differences in these texts represent, in a sense, the essence of theater: the texts of plays were initially not intended for publication. They were scripts, designed for the actors to perform – the principal life of the play at this period was in performance. And it follows that in Shakespeare's theater the playwright typically had no say either in how his play was performed or in the disposition of his text – he was an employee of the company. The authoritative figures in the theatrical enterprise were the shareholders in the company, who were for the most part the major actors. They decided what plays were to be done; they hired the playwright and often gave him an outline of the play they wanted him to write. Often, too, the play was a collaboration: the company would retain a group of writers, and parcel out the scenes among them. The resulting script was then the property of the company, and the actors would revise it as they saw fit during the course of putting it on stage. The resulting text belonged to the company. The playwright had no rights in it once he had been paid. (This system survives largely intact in the movie industry, and most of the playwrights of Shakespeare's time were as anonymous as most screenwriters are today.) The script could also, of course, continue to change as the tastes of audiences and the requirements of the actors changed. Many – perhaps most – plays were revised when they were reintroduced after any substantial absence from the repertory, or when they were performed by a company different from the one that originally commissioned the play.

Shakespeare was an exceptional figure in this world because he was not only a shareholder and actor in his company, but also its leading playwright – he was literally his own boss. He had, moreover, little interest in the publication of his plays, and even those that appeared during his lifetime with the authorization of the company show no signs of any editorial concern on the part of the author. Theater was, for Shakespeare, a fluid and supremely responsive medium – the very opposite of the great classic canonical text that has embodied his works since 1623.

The very fluidity of the original texts, however, has meant that Shakespeare has always had to be edited. Here is an example of how problematic the editorial project inevitably is, a passage from the most famous speech in *Romeo and Juliet*, Juliet's balcony soliloquy beginning "O Romeo, Romeo, wherefore art thou Romeo?" Since the eighteenth century, the standard modern text has read,

> What's Montague? It is nor hand, nor foot,
> Nor arm, nor face, nor any other part
> Belonging to a man. O be some other name!
> What's in a name? That which we call a rose
> By any other name would smell as sweet.
>
> (II.2.40-44)

Editors have three early texts of this play to work from, two quarto texts and the folio. Here is how the First Quarto (1597) reads:

> Whats *Mountague?* It is nor hand nor foote,
> Nor arme, nor face, nor any other part.
> Whats in a name? That which we call a Rofe,
> By any other name would fmell as fweet:

Here is the Second Quarto (1599):

> Whats *Mountague?* it is nor hand nor foote,
> Nor arme nor face, ô be fome other name
> Belonging to a man.
> Whats in a name that which we call a rofe,
> By any other word would fmell as fweete,

And here is the First Folio (1623):

> What's *Mountague?* it is nor hand nor foote,
> Nor arme, nor face, O be fome other name
> Belonging to a man.
> What? in a names that which we call a Rofe,
> By any other word would fmell as fweete,

There is in fact no early text that reads as our modern text does – and this is the most famous speech in the play. Instead, we have three quite different texts, all of which are clearly some version of the same speech, but none of which seems to us a final or satisfactory version. The transcendently beautiful passage in modern editions is an editorial invention: editors have succeeded in conflating and revising the three versions into something we recognize as great poetry. Is this what Shakespeare "really" wrote? Who can say? What we can say is that Shakespeare always had performance, not a book, in mind.

Books About the Shakespeare Texts

The standard study of the printing history of the First Folio is W. W. Greg, *The Shakespeare First Folio* (1955). J. K. Walton, *The Quarto Copy for the First Folio of Shakespeare*

(1971), is a useful survey of the relation of the quartos to the folio. The second edition of Charlton Hinman's *Norton Facsimile* of the First Folio (1996), with a new introduction by Peter Blayney, is indispensable. Stanley Wells, Gary Taylor, John Jowett, and William Montgomery, *William Shakespeare: A Textual Companion,* keyed to the Oxford text, gives a comprehensive survey of the editorial situation for all the plays and poems.

THE GENERAL EDITORS

Introduction

MODERN CRITICISM HAS HAD a difficult time accommodating *The Taming of the Shrew* to the models we have wanted Shakespeare to provide for us of the relations between the sexes, but attempts to rescue the play from charges of sexism have been halfhearted at best, and are, in any case, historically uninformed. Shakespeare here participates in an ongoing debate throughout the early modern era about the place of women within the patriarchal system, and one of the greatest pleasures the play would have provided for a Renaissance audience certainly lay in its conviction that a shrewish woman could indeed be successfully managed. The play would also doubtless have been seen as a fairy tale, but the pleasure would have been no less acute for that. Critics wishing to recuperate Shakespeare for the cause of feminism can take comfort in the fact that the playwright was at least not discriminatory: Portia in *The Merchant of Venice* and Paulina in *The Winter's Tale* offer equally sexist object lessons to wives on the management of their husbands.

The critical discomfort has been more easily dealt with in the performing tradition – often, to be sure, through radical revision – and the play, in one form or another, has had a continuous success on the stage as far back as our records will take us. It seems, in fact, never to have been out of the repertory. Though few Shakespeare plays were still being presented in Caroline England, it remained popular enough to be performed at court in 1633 (which means that it must have been actively in the repertory). With the reopening of the playhouses after the Restoration, it was one of the classic plays regularly performed by Thomas Killigrew's King's Company. Samuel

Pepys went to see it in 1667, and recorded in his diary that he found it "but a mean play" with, however, "some very good pieces in it" – he also complained of difficulty understanding Shakespeare's language. Nevertheless, he and his wife went to see the play again six months later – this time he declared it simply "a silly play and an old one." Killigrew soon had the play refurbished by the actor-playwright John Lacy, who retitled it *Sauny the Scot,* set it in contemporary London, transformed Katherine to Margaret, and renamed all the main characters except Petruchio. He thoroughly modernized the language, and starred in it as Petruchio's servant Grumio, renamed Sauny. As this indicates, Lacy's version included a good deal of new material, but the play is recognizably *The Taming of the Shrew.* Thereafter it went through a further series of metamorphoses. By 1715 the London stage was presenting two farces based entirely on the Christopher Sly episodes, both called *The Cobbler of Preston.* In 1735 a version of the play appeared at Drury Lane under the title *A Cure for a Scold.* In 1756 Garrick revised and revived it as *Catherine and Petruchio* with great success, and this was the form in which John Philip Kemble played it at Covent Garden in 1806. In 1828 an operatic version of the play was performed. It was not until 1844, at the Haymarket Theatre, that the original text, including the Sly scenes, was returned to the London stage, by J. R. Planché, who had pioneered historically authentic costuming in the production of Shakespearean drama. This was not only a return to Shakespeare; it was a return to Shakespearean staging: the play was done essentially without scenery, on an open stage, and with only hangings and screens. After this, the original text – though not always including Sly, and often with a significant mitigation of Katherine's final capitulation – survived in the theater more or less intact.

Kate and Petruchio have always been irresistible roles, not least for husband and wife teams, and not always for artistic reasons. In the twentieth century, Sybil Thorndike and Lewis Casson, and Alfred Lunt and Lynn Fontanne were notable successes in the play. The only film Mary Pickford and Douglas Fairbanks made together, in 1929, one of the first talking films for either, was a quite wooden but very successful *Taming of the Shrew* – despite the stars' obvious ineptitude at speaking Shakespearean verse, audiences loved seeing the most famous couple in Hollywood going at each other at a time when the gossip columnists revealed that their marriage was falling apart. And Franco Zeffirelli's handsome 1966 film starring Richard Burton and Elizabeth Taylor made the roles appear to have been written for the notorious, glamorous, squabbling pair.

The story of the taming of Katherine by Petruchio, however, is not the whole play – in a sense, it is not the play at all. *The Taming of the Shrew* begins as a play about a drunken beggar, Christopher Sly, on whom a lord decides to play a joke. Dressing Sly, in his drunken stupor, in rich garments, providing him with servants and even a boy actor claiming to be his wife, the lord persuades Sly that he is an amnesiac aristocrat. The play *The Taming of the Shrew* is a play within this play, a performance enacted for Sly's entertainment. Sly has never seen a play before, and for the first two scenes he is a willing enough spectator, though he would clearly rather go to bed with his "wife"; but by the end of Act I, scene 2 he declares himself thoroughly bored. The play nevertheless continues, apparently with Sly a mute, and possibly sleeping, onstage audience. And he is never heard from or mentioned again; he presumably remains onstage, but, to the perennial despair of directors, Shakespeare completely ignores him – the play within the play becomes the play. What happens to Christopher Sly? In another version of the play, called *The Taming of a Shrew* (published in 1594, and almost certainly deriving from Shakespeare's play, not the other way round), there is a concluding scene with Sly, now returned to his senses and to his own person, who heads for home declaring that he has learned from the play within the play how to tame his own wife. It is certainly possible that this was how Shakespeare originally ended his comedy; but if so, he apparently thought better of it. The loose end was, for Shakespeare, a second thought and an improvement.

It also makes the play, of course, a major anomaly, not only in Shakespeare's career, but in drama generally. There are many other plays within plays – Shakespeare was to use the metatheatrical device again in *A Midsummer Night's Dream, As You Like It, Hamlet,* and *The Tempest,* to name only the most notable examples; but there is no other play in which the interpolated entertainment utterly abolishes its frame, and becomes the play itself. The play of the same period that most resembles it in this respect is Francis Beaumont's *The Knight of the Burning Pestle* (c. 1607). In this, an audience assembles onstage to see a play called *The London Merchant.* As the actor speaking the prologue begins, he is interrupted by a grocer in the audience named George, who is offended by the satiric treatment of the merchant classes in London plays, and assumes that *The London Merchant* will be similarly offensive. Unmoved by the reassurances of the speaker of the prologue, George calls for a heroic drama about the middle class, and at his insistence his apprentice Rafe is introduced onto the stage to perform the chivalric epic *The Knight of the Burning Pestle,* scenes of which are interspersed with *The London Merchant,* while the grocer and his wife act as a critical chorus throughout. Here, despite the fact that the play takes its title from the interpolated drama, the frame story never disappears – it is, indeed, the controlling element of the play – and the grocer, his wife, and Rafe are the most fully developed characters in the drama. Shakespeare's dramaturgy is far more radical. He may, of course, simply have lost interest in Christopher Sly and the mischievous lord of his frame story; but *The Taming of the Shrew* can also be viewed as Shakespeare's dramatic testimony, in the first years of his career, to the reality of fictions and the power of theater.

The Taming of the Shrew was written somewhere between 1590 and 1594 (it was not printed until the 1623 folio, though it then proved popular enough with readers to warrant its republication, in a separate quarto in 1631). At this time the nation had been ruled by a powerful and articulate woman, with notable success, for almost four decades. Elizabeth had, moreover, succeeded another woman, her half sister Mary, on the throne. These were the first queens ever to rule in their own right in England. Their accession was remarkable not only because they were women, but even more because both had been declared illegitimate on the birth of their half brother Edward, who succeeded Henry VIII as Edward VI. Mary was automatically delegitimized when her father's marriage to her mother, Katherine of Aragon, was annulled; Elizabeth's legitimacy was a casualty of her mother's, Anne Boleyn's, conviction and execution on charges of adultery and incest. Both remained in the line of succession only because Henry VIII had included them as a fail-safe provision in his will, in the unlikely event that Edward would die without heirs.

The fact that Henry's will was adhered to when the unlikely event took place, even though the accession of Mary necessitated returning the country to Roman Catholicism, probably says more about the overwhelming desire for an orderly succession than about any conviction that Henry's daughters were likely to be good rulers. Possibly it was felt that as women, they could be managed, just as Edward, who came to the throne as a child of ten and died six years later, had been manageable. In any case, one of the first acts of Mary's rule was the formal declaration that, for legal purposes, she was a man. This is a good index to the culture's assumptions about where authority legitimately resides, and what its gender is – though the fact that a means could be found to allow it legally to reside in a woman is also to the point. Elizabeth never considered this legal strategy necessary, but she was fond of playing off her female person against her masculine spirit, as in her famous remark in the Armada speech to the army at Tilbury in 1588, on the eve of a projected Spanish invasion: "I have the body of a weak and feeble woman, but the heart and spirit of a king, and a king of England too."

Perhaps even more inflammatory than the issue of women's rights and prerogatives was the question of parental control over marriage. At the time the play was written, the age of consent was twelve for women, fourteen for men; this is the age at which a contract could legally be entered into – in this case, the contract of marriage. But children were also legally their father's property, and the right to dispose of the child in marriage was a property right. Daughters were particularly valuable pieces of disposable property: for fathers because they represented potential alliances with rich and powerful families, for prospective fathers- and sons-in-law because they came accompanied with dowries. For a daughter to negotiate her own marriage by eloping or marrying secretly (like Desdemona or Juliet) was tantamount to theft. The fact that at the age of twelve she was legally entitled to do so was a continual cause of complaint and debate; and in practice, the age of consent often meant only that a daughter could not be forced to consent to a marriage before she reached the age of twelve. In 1604 the forces of patriarchy were greatly strengthened when the age of consent was raised to twenty-one, thereby significantly increasing paternal control over marriage.

The idea of a rich man's daughter deliberately rendering herself unmarriageable through her antisocial behavior, therefore, has a good deal of cultural resonance in the England of 1590. But Shakespeare seriously loads Katherine's case in ways that have little to do with Elizabethan law or practice. In Elizabethan law, a declaration of intention to marry in the presence of witnesses constituted a valid betrothal, which was an enforceable contract; and the pronouncing of vows in the presence of witnesses constituted a common-law marriage. Neither of these conditions, however, is fulfilled in the case of Katherine and Petruchio. Katherine does not declare herself a willing bride – quite the contrary. What is, in fact, most striking about the marriage in the context of both Elizabethan social history and the early scenes of Katherine's behavior in the household is that she almost immediately accedes to it. For all her famous temper, she turns out to be remarkably pliable, doing exactly as her father – and sister, and sister's suitors, and Petruchio – wish her to do.

Her younger sister, Bianca, on the surface all sweetness and good nature, is in fact the willful one, getting what she wants by pretending to be pliable. In a sense the taming of Katherine consists of turning her into Bianca – revealing to Katherine that she can get what she wants out of her husband by simply telling him what he wants to hear. In fact the only thing unusual about Katherine the shrew is that she is a shrew when she is unmarried. The shrew after marriage, the shrewish wife, is almost a convention of the drama of Shakespeare's age. And Katherine's shrewishness is problematic precisely because it renders her unmarriageable; she is a piece of her father's disposable property, and she is preventing him from disposing of her. It is clear that there are no other options than marriage for women in these dramas.

What would render a woman unmarriageable in this world? Nothing, really, but lack of money. Consider the case of Mariana in *Measure for Measure*, betrothed to Angelo, but abandoned by him when it turns out that she will have no dowry. Angelo's behavior is caddish, certainly, but only because betrothal constitutes a legal contract. Had Mariana's money disappeared before the engagement, Angelo's loss of interest would be both comprehensible and entirely acceptable. By the same token, in

The Merchant of Venice all the suitors making their way to Belmont, including the romantic hero Bassanio, want to marry Portia because she is "a lady richly left" (I.1.161) – her fortune, indeed, is the first thing Bassanio mentions in describing her virtues to his friend Antonio. Grace, beauty, wit, good conversation are all admirable traits in Shakespeare's women, but they are nothing without a sufficient dowry. And Petruchio is willing, indeed eager, to marry Katherine because, whatever her character, she brings money with her – one of the reasons for marrying in Shakespeare's world was to repair or augment one's fortunes. This is not necessarily the only reason; but it is nevertheless a compelling and, as in the case of Petruchio, often a sufficient one: "I come to wive it wealthily in Padua – / If wealthily, then happily in Padua" (I.2.74-75). There are, in contrast, perfectly presentable but nevertheless unmarriageable men in Shakespeare – the two Antonios of *The Merchant of Venice* and *Twelfth Night,* Don Pedro in *Much Ado About Nothing,* even, apparently, the duke in *Measure for Measure* (who offers marriage to Isabella and, within the play, at least, receives no answer) – but the fifteen percent of early-seventeenth-century upper-class daughters who, according to Lawrence Stone's statistics, never married find no place in Shakespeare's dramatic world.* There are widows in Shakespeare, but no spinsters or old maids.

Katherine is wooed by bullying, invective, and physical mistreatment, Bianca by impersonation, rhetoric, and charm; but in fact the two suitors' methods have more in common than appears on the surface. Petruchio's means of reducing Katherine to a wife are hardly subtle, but they depend as much on misrepresentation, costume, and play-acting as does Lucentio's wooing of Bianca. Convincing Katherine that she has married a lunatic is a matter of the wrong clothes, the wrong horse wrongly caparisoned,

---

* *The Family, Sex, and Marriage* (New York: Harper, 1979), p. 40.

the wrong names for familiar objects. Training Katherine to deal with the lunatic on his own terms, however, is a much more physical business, involving hunger and sleep deprivation; and nothing in the play questions Petruchio's right to torture his wife in this way. Nor is the disciplinary theater confined to Petruchio: his servants become a troupe of actors participating in the charade, and even the ill-used tailor, who supplies a dress perfectly designed according to Petruchio's orders and then is berated for his incompetence, is subsequently silently paid off. In the world Shakespeare imagines, Katherine is without allies or even sympathetic bystanders.

Nevertheless, though there is no way of making Shakespeare into a proto-feminist, the play has its subversive elements. Katherine's energy, resilience, and individuality render her a character that three centuries of notably independent and attractive actresses have wanted to play – outside the fiction, she has a world of admirers and allies. Even in the play's terms, she is at the very least a worthy adversary in a battle that the history of patriarchy rendered unequal; and if we look forward a few years to *Much Ado About Nothing,* we may say that Beatrice more than holds her own with Benedick because Katherine has shown Shakespeare how to enable her to do so. But more subtly than this, Petruchio and Lucentio are successful in their wooing because they alone of the suitors acknowledge that there is more to life than patriarchy – that marriages cannot simply be arranged, that whatever fathers agree to, wooing is a hands-on business. The degree of disguise, misrepresentation, and playacting that both their suits require is a measure of precisely how subversive such an assumption is to patriarchal values.

Nor is it even clear that Lucentio's success with Bianca constitutes a happy ending within the patriarchal system. When the marriage is revealed to her father, Baptista, instead of offering his blessing he merely resolves "to sound the depth of this knavery" (V.1.127), and Lucentio's father, Vincentio, swears vengeance on Tranio, the hapless servant whom his son has employed to manage his romantic fraud. All that is satisfied in these conclusions is the appearance of normalcy: whatever Kate feels in her heart, she publicly declares herself an obedient wife; though Bianca is ignoring her father's authority, she nominally obtains his consent to her marriage. The play's resolution, in fact, may be seen as a version of the Elizabethan Settlement, the compromise Elizabeth succeeded in negotiating among the various religious factions of her realm, whereby what was required of all subjects was outward conformity, but so long as the externals were observed – regular attendance at church, the execution of the oath of allegiance – the question of belief was not at issue.

Perhaps the best epitome of the fortunes of this very popular but disquieting and endlessly amended play over the past four hundred years is provided by the work in which it has had its most widespread modern success, Sam and Bella Spewak and Cole Porter's great *Kiss Me Kate,* a musical about a troupe of actors always about to perform, or in the midst of performing, or having just finished performing *The Taming of the Shrew.* We never quite see the play. We see the actors, and the preparations, and some bits of various scenes; but the full implications of Shakespeare's comedy are assumed to be a little more than we can handle.

STEPHEN ORGEL
Stanford University

Note on the Text

THE TAMING OF THE SHREW was first published in the folio of 1623. It was apparently printed from Shakespeare's working manuscript, before its transcription into a promptbook. The folio text is not divided into scenes, and its act division requires amendment. In F, the induction is labeled I.1, and Acts I and II are not indicated. Acts III, IV, and V begin, respectively, at what modern editions call III.1, IV.3, and V.2. Substantive departures from the folio text are listed below; the reading adopted is in italics, the folio reading in roman.

Ind.1 1 s.d. *Christophero Sly* (in F at end of s.d.)   5 *pocas palabras* Paucas pallabris   15 *Breathe* Brach   **20, 28** *FIRST HUNTSMAN* Hunts.   **81** *A PLAYER* 2. Player   **87** *A PLAYER* Sincklo   **99** *A PLAYER* Plai   **136** *their* the

Ind.2 2 *lordship* Lord   25 *it is* is it   91 *Greet* Greece   134 *play it. Is not* play, it is not

I.1 3 *in* for   13 *Vincentio* Vincentio's   42 *now were* thou wert   47 **s.d.** *suitor* sister   128 *her faults* faults   159 *captum* captam   241 *your* you   245 **s.d.** *speak* speakes

I.2 18 *masters* mistris   72 *she* she is   119 *me and other* me. Other   133 *last* least   151 *go. What* go to: what   170 *help me* helpe one   195 *he'll* Ile   206 *th' ear* heare   211 *ours* yours   222 *to woo?* to –   248 *as to ask* as aske   250 *I do hear* heare I do   264 *feat* seeke

II.1 3 *gawds* goods   8 *charge thee* charge   31 *Will* What will   75–76 *wooing. Neighbor, this* wooing neighbors: this   79 *unto you* vnto   169 *I will* Ile; **s.d.** (in F after l. 168)   181 **s.d.** (in F after l. 183)   254 *a* the   271 *upon* on   331 *in* me   345 *have Bianca's* haue my Biancas

III.1 47 *How . . . is* (F heads line *Luc.*)   50 *BIANCA* (F omits)   51 *LUCENTIO* Bian.   53 *BIANCA* Hort.   80 *change* charge; *odd* old   81 *MESSENGER* Nicke

III.2 29 *of thy* of   30 *master, old* master,   54 *swayed* Waid   58 *new-repaired* now repaired   126 *sir, to* sir,   128 *As I* As   147 *come* came   157 *Did* Should   177–78 *echo. / I* eccho: and I   209 *nor till* not till   249 *you supply* you shall supply

IV.1 10 **s.d.** *a Servant* (in F in l. 170 s.d.)   37 *thou wilt* wilt thou   42 *and white* the white   56 *is* 'tis   129 *Food, food, food, food* Soud, soud, soud,

soud   167 *in* for   170 **s.d.** *Enter Curtis* Enter Curtis a Servant (in F after l. 171)

IV.2 4 *HORTENSIO* Luc.   6 *LUCENTIO* Hor.   8 *LUCENTIO* Hor.   13 *none* me   31 *her* them   63 *mercatante* Mercantant   71 *Take in* Take me (F heads line *Par.*)   86 *are newly* are but newly   92 *thus* this

IV.3 81 *is a* is   85 *I will have it* it I will haue   88 *like a* like   96 *I* and   178 *account'st* accountedst

IV.4 **s.d.** *booted and* (in F in l. 18 s.d.)   1 *Sir* Sirs   6 *TRANIO* (in F heads l. 5)   18 **s.d.** *Pedant bareheaded* Pedant booted and bare headed   19 *Signor . . . met* (F heads line *Tra.*)   68 *Dally . . . gone* (after this line F adds *Enter Peter*)   90 *except* expect   92 *with* take   101 *ready against* readie to come against

IV.5 18 *is* in   22 *still* so   26 *soft, what company* soft, Company   35 *a* the   37 *where* whether   77 *she be* she

V.1 5 *master* mistris   28 *Pisa* Padua   28–29 *and is here* and here   48 *master's* Mistris   49 *my* my old   76 *Lucentio. He* Lucentio, and he   100 *spoiled, yonder* spoil'd, and yonder   141 *never's* neuer

V.2 2 *done* come   23 *Conceive* Conceiues   57 *O ho* Oh, Oh   65 *for* sir   128 *the* that   134 *a* fiue

The Taming of the Shrew

[NAMES OF THE ACTORS

In the induction:

A LORD, *later posing as a servant*
CHRISTOPHER SLY
BARTHOLOMEW, *page to the Lord, posing as Sly's wife*
A COMPANY OF STROLLING PLAYERS
HUNTSMEN AND SERVANTS TO THE LORD
HOSTESS OF A TAVERN

In the play proper:

BAPTISTA MINOLA, *father to Kate and Bianca*
VINCENTIO, *father to Lucentio*
GREMIO, *a pantaloon, a suitor to Bianca*
LUCENTIO, *in love with Bianca, later posing as Cambio*
HORTENSIO, *suitor to Bianca, later posing as Litio*
PETRUCHIO, *suitor to Kate*
A PEDANT, *later posing as Vincentio*
TRANIO, *servant to Lucentio, later posing as Lucentio*
BIONDELLO, *page to Lucentio*
GRUMIO, *servant to Petruchio*
CURTIS, *servant to Petruchio*
A TAILOR
A HABERDASHER
KATHERINE (KATE), *the shrew*
BIANCA
A WIDOW
SERVANTS *to Baptista, Petruchio, Lucentio*

SCENE: *Warwickshire; Padua; near Verona*]

*

The Taming of the Shrew

[INDUCTION]

❧ **Ind.1** *Enter Beggar (Christophero Sly) and Hostess.*

SLY   I'll feeze you, in faith.   1

HOSTESS   A pair of stocks, you rogue!   2

SLY   You're a baggage, the Slys are no rogues. Look in the
chronicles: we came in with Richard Conqueror.   4
Therefore *pocas palabras,* let the world slide. Sessa!   5

HOSTESS   You will not pay for the glasses you have burst?   6

SLY   No, not a denier. Go by, Saint Jeronimy, go to thy   7
cold bed and warm thee.

HOSTESS   I know my remedy: I must go fetch the head-   9
borough.   *[Exit.]*   10

SLY   Third or fourth or fifth borough, I'll answer him by
law. I'll not budge an inch, boy: let him come, and   12
kindly.   13

Induction, scene 1 A country inn   **1** *feeze* fix   **2** *A . . . stocks* (she threatens
to have him put in the stocks)   **4** *Richard Conqueror* (Sly's error for William
the Conqueror)   **5** *pocas palabras* few words (Spanish); *let . . . slide* (proverbial: "forget it"); *Sessa* shut up, stop it (perhaps from French *cessez*)   **6** *burst*
broken   **7** *denier* French copper coin of little value; *Go . . . Jeronimy* i.e., forget it (Sly misquotes a famous line from Kyd's *The Spanish Tragedy,*
"Hieronymo beware, go by, go by," III.12.30, mistaking the hero of the play
for Saint Jerome)   **9–10** *headborough* constable (the alternative term was
"thirdborough," hence Sly's reply)   **12** *boy* (an interjection, not addressed to
anyone)

Falls asleep.
Wind horns. Enter a Lord from hunting, with his train.

LORD
14 Huntsman, I charge thee, tender well my hounds.
15 Breathe Merriman, the poor cur is embossed,
16 And couple Clowder with the deep-mouthed brach.
Saw'st thou not, boy, how Silver made it good
18 At the hedge corner in the coldest fault?
I would not lose the dog for twenty pound.

FIRST HUNTSMAN
20 Why Bellman is as good as he, my lord.
21 He cried upon it at the merest loss
And twice today picked out the dullest scent.
Trust me, I take him for the better dog.

LORD
24 Thou art a fool. If Echo were as fleet,
I would esteem him worth a dozen such.
But sup them well and look unto them all.
Tomorrow I intend to hunt again.

FIRST HUNTSMAN
I will, my lord.

LORD
What's here? One dead or drunk? See, doth he breathe?

SECOND HUNTSMAN
30 He breathes, my lord. Were he not warmed with ale
This were a bed but cold to sleep so soundly.

LORD
O monstrous beast, how like a swine he lies!
Grim death, how foul and loathsome is thine image!
34 Sirs, I will practice on this drunken man.

---

13 s.d. *Wind* sound   14 *tender* care for   15 *Breathe* rest; *embossed* exhausted
16 *couple* leash together; *deep-mouthed* with a deep bark; *brach* bitch   18
in . . . fault even though the scent was cold   21 *cried . . . loss* barked to show
that he had picked up the scent after it had been utterly lost   24 *fleet* swift
34 *practice* play a trick

What think you, if he were conveyed to bed,
Wrapped in sweet clothes, rings put upon his fingers,   36
A most delicious banquet by his bed,
And brave attendants near him when he wakes,   38
Would not the beggar then forget himself?

FIRST HUNTSMAN
Believe me, lord, I think he cannot choose.   40

SECOND HUNTSMAN
It would seem strange unto him when he waked.

LORD
Even as a flatt'ring dream or worthless fancy.
Then take him up and manage well the jest.
Carry him gently to my fairest chamber
And hang it round with all my wanton pictures.
Balm his foul head in warm distillèd waters
And burn sweet wood to make the lodging sweet.
Procure me music ready when he wakes
To make a dulcet and a heavenly sound.
And if he chance to speak be ready straight,   50
And with a low submissive reverence
Say, "What is it your honor will command?"
Let one attend him with a silver basin
Full of rose water and bestrewed with flowers,
Another bear the ewer, the third a diaper,   55
And say, "Will't please your lordship cool your hands?"
Some one be ready with a costly suit
And ask him what apparel he will wear,
Another tell him of his hounds and horse
And that his lady mourns at his disease.   60
Persuade him that he hath been lunatic,
And when he says he is, say that he dreams,   62
For he is nothing but a mighty lord.

---

36 *sweet* perfumed 38 *brave* finely dressed 50 *straight* immediately 55
diaper linen towel 62 *is* i.e., must be lunatic

64 This do, and do it kindly, gentle sirs.
65 It will be pastime passing excellent,
66 If it be husbanded with modesty.

FIRST HUNTSMAN
    My lord, I warrant you we will play our part,
68 As he shall think, by our true diligence,
    He is no less than what we say he is.

LORD
70 Take him up gently, and to bed with him,
    And each one to his office when he wakes.
                    [Sly is carried out.] Sound trumpets.
72 Sirrah, go see what trumpet 'tis that sounds.
                    [Exit Servingman.]
73 Belike some noble gentleman that means,
    Traveling some journey, to repose him here.
        Enter Servingman.
    How now, who is it?

SERVINGMAN
76 An't please your honor, players
    That offer service to your lordship.
        Enter Players.

LORD
    Bid them come near. – Now, fellows, you are welcome.

PLAYERS
    We thank your honor.

LORD
80 Do you intend to stay with me tonight?

A PLAYER
81 So please your lordship to accept our duty.

LORD
    With all my heart. This fellow I remember

---

64 *kindly* naturally   65 *passing* surpassingly   66 *husbanded* managed; *modesty* moderation   68 *As* so that   72 *Sirrah* (usual form of address to an inferior)   73 *Belike* probably   76 *An't* if it   81 *duty* service

Since once he played a farmer's eldest son.
'Twas where you wooed the gentlewoman so well.
I have forgot your name, but sure that part
Was aptly fitted and naturally performed.

A PLAYER

I think 'twas Soto that your honor means.

LORD

'Tis very true, thou didst it excellent.
Well, you are come to me in happy time,   89
The rather for I have some sport in hand   90
Wherein your cunning can assist me much.   91
There is a lord will hear you play tonight;
But I am doubtful of your modesties,   93
Lest, overeyeing of his odd behavior –   94
For yet his honor never heard a play –
You break into some merry passion   96
And so offend him; for I tell you, sirs,
If you should smile he grows impatient.

A PLAYER

Fear not, my lord, we can contain ourselves
Were he the veriest antic in the world.   100

LORD

Go, sirrah, take them to the buttery   101
And give them friendly welcome every one.
Let them want nothing that my house affords.
                              Exit one with the Players.
Sirrah, go you to Barthol'mew my page   104
And see him dressed in all suits like a lady.   105
That done, conduct him to the drunkard's chamber
And call him madam; do him obeisance.
Tell him from me – as he will win my love –

---

89 *happy* opportune   **91** *cunning* skill   **93** *modesties* discretion   **94** *overeyeing of* witnessing   **96** *merry passion* laughing fit   **100** *veriest antic* greatest buffoon   **101** *buttery* larder   **104** *Barthol'mew* (pronounced "Bartlemy")   **105** *suits* respects

He bear himself with honorable action
110 Such as he hath observed in noble ladies
111 Unto their lords, by them accomplishèd.
Such duty to the drunkard let him do
113 With soft low tongue and lowly courtesy,
And say, "What is't your honor will command
Wherein your lady and your humble wife
May show her duty and make known her love?"
And then with kind embracements, tempting kisses,
And with declining head into his bosom,
Bid him shed tears, as being overjoyed
120 To see her noble lord restored to health
121 Who for this seven years hath esteemed him
No better than a poor and loathsome beggar.
And if the boy have not a woman's gift
To rain a shower of commanded tears,
125 An onion will do well for such a shift,
126 Which in a napkin being close conveyed
Shall in despite enforce a watery eye.
See this dispatched with all the haste thou canst:
129 Anon I'll give thee more instructions.

Exit a Servingman.

130 I know the boy will well usurp the grace,
Voice, gait, and action of a gentlewoman.
I long to hear him call the drunkard husband,
And how my men will stay themselves from laughter
When they do homage to this simple peasant.
I'll in to counsel them; haply my presence
136 May well abate their overmerry spleen
Which otherwise would grow into extremes. *[Exeunt.]*

✳

---

111 *accomplishèd* performed 113 *lowly courtesy* humble curtsy 121 *esteemed him* considered himself 125 *shift* purpose 126 *napkin* handkerchief; *close* secretly 129 *Anon* shortly 130 *usurp* assume 136 *spleen* mood

∽ **Ind.2** *Enter aloft the Drunkard [Sly] with Attendants, some with apparel, basin and ewer, and other appurtenances; and Lord [as a Servant].*

SLY   For God's sake, a pot of small ale.   1

FIRST SERVINGMAN
   Will't please your lordship drink a cup of sack?   2

SECOND SERVINGMAN
   Will't please your honor taste of these conserves?   3

THIRD SERVINGMAN
   What raiment will your honor wear today?

SLY   I am Christophero Sly, call not me honor nor lordship. I ne'er drank sack in my life, and if you give me
   any conserves, give me conserves of beef. Ne'er ask me   7
   what raiment I'll wear, for I have no more doublets   8
   than backs, no more stockings than legs, nor no more
   shoes than feet; nay, sometime more feet than shoes, or   10
   such shoes as my toes look through the overleather.

LORD
   Heaven cease this idle humor in your honor!   12
   O that a mighty man of such descent,
   Of such possessions and so high esteem,
   Should be infusèd with so foul a spirit!

SLY   What, would you make me mad? Am not I Christopher Sly, old Sly's son of Burton-heath, by birth a ped-   17
   dler, by education a cardmaker, by transmutation a   18
   bearherd, and now by present profession a tinker? Ask   19

Induction, scene 2 The lord's manor house   **s.d.** *aloft* i.e., in the tiring-house gallery over the stage (Capell, 1768, supplied a stage direction calling for a bed and other stage properties, but l. 35 makes clear that a bed was not used in the original staging)   **1** *small* weak (hence cheap)   **2** *sack* sherry (a gentleman's drink)   **3** *conserves* candied fruit   **7** *conserves of beef* salt beef   **8** *doublets* coats   **12** *humor* obsession   **17** *Burton-heath* Barton-on-the-Heath (a village near Stratford)   **18** *cardmaker* (a card was a comb used in preparing wool for spinning)   **19** *bearherd* keeper of a tame bear; *tinker* itinerant pot mender (proverbially a hard drinker)

20 Marian Hacket, the fat alewife of Wincot, if she know
21 me not. If she say I am not fourteen pence on the score
22 for sheer ale, score me up for the lyingest knave in
23 Christendom. What, I am not bestraught: here's –

THIRD SERVINGMAN
O this it is that makes your lady mourn.

SECOND SERVINGMAN
O this it is that makes your servants droop.

LORD
Hence comes it that your kindred shuns your house,
As beaten hence by your strange lunacy.
O noble lord, bethink thee of thy birth,
29 Call home thy ancient thoughts from banishment
30 And banish hence these abject lowly dreams.
Look how thy servants do attend on thee,
Each in his office ready at thy beck.
33 Wilt thou have music? Hark, Apollo plays,
  Music.
And twenty cagèd nightingales do sing.
Or wilt thou sleep? We'll have thee to a couch
Softer and sweeter than the lustful bed
37 On purpose trimmed up for Semiramis.
38 Say thou wilt walk, we will bestrew the ground.
39 Or wilt thou ride? Thy horses shall be trapped,
40 Their harness studded all with gold and pearl.
Dost thou love hawking? Thou hast hawks will soar
Above the morning lark. Or wilt thou hunt?
43 Thy hounds shall make the welkin answer them
And fetch shrill echoes from the hollow earth.

FIRST SERVINGMAN
45 Say thou wilt course, thy greyhounds are as swift

---

20 *Wincot* a hamlet four miles southwest of Stratford (Hackets were living in the parish in 1591)   21 *on the score* chalked up as owing   22 *sheer* unmixed; *score me up for* write me down as   23 *bestraught* distraught, mad   29 *ancient* former   33 *Apollo* god of music   37 *Semiramis* notoriously lustful queen of Assyria   38 *bestrew* spread carpets on   39 *trapped* adorned   43 *welkin* sky   45 *course* hunt hares

As breathèd stags, ay, fleeter than the roe.   46
SECOND SERVINGMAN
   Dost thou love pictures? We will fetch thee straight
   Adonis painted by a running brook   48
   And Cytherea all in sedges hid,   49
   Which seem to move and wanton with her breath   50
   Even as the waving sedges play with wind.
LORD
   We'll show thee Io as she was a maid   52
   And how she was beguilèd and surprised,
   As lively painted as the deed was done.   54
THIRD SERVINGMAN
   Or Daphne roaming through a thorny wood,   55
   Scratching her legs that one shall swear she bleeds,
   And at that sight shall sad Apollo weep,
   So workmanly the blood and tears are drawn.
LORD
   Thou art a lord and nothing but a lord.
   Thou hast a lady far more beautiful   60
   Than any woman in this waning age.   61
FIRST SERVINGMAN
   And till the tears that she hath shed for thee
   Like envious floods o'errun her lovely face   63
   She was the fairest creature in the world,
   And yet she is inferior to none.   65
SLY
   Am I a lord, and have I such a lady?
   Or do I dream? Or have I dreamed till now?
   I do not sleep: I see, I hear, I speak,

---

46 *breathèd* in good wind; *roe* small deer   48 *Adonis* (loved by Venus and
killed by a wild boar while hunting; cf. Shakespeare's *Venus and Adonis*)   49
Cytherea Venus (associated with the island of Cythera); *sedges* water rushes
50 *wanton* sway seductively   52 *Io* (loved by Jupiter in the shape of a cloud
and changed by him into a heifer to deceive the jealous Juno)   54 *lively* en-
ergetically   55 *Daphne* (wooed by Apollo and changed into a laurel tree to
escape his pursuit)   61 *waning* degenerate   63 *envious* hateful   65 *yet* even
now

I smell sweet savors and I feel soft things.

70 Upon my life, I am a lord indeed,
And not a tinker nor Christopher Sly.
Well, bring our lady hither to our sight,
73 And once again, a pot o' th' smallest ale.

SECOND SERVINGMAN
Will't please your mightiness to wash your hands?
75 O how we joy to see your wit restored.
O that once more you knew but what you are!
These fifteen years you have been in a dream,
Or when you waked, so waked as if you slept.

SLY
79 These fifteen years? By my fay, a goodly nap.
80 But did I never speak of all that time?

FIRST SERVINGMAN
O yes, my lord, but very idle words,
For though you lay here in this goodly chamber,
Yet would you say ye were beaten out of door
84 And rail upon the hostess of the house,
85 And say you would present her at the leet
86 Because she brought stone jugs and no sealed quarts.
87 Sometimes you would call out for Cicely Hacket.

SLY
Ay, the woman's maid of the house.

THIRD SERVINGMAN
Why, sir, you know no house nor no such maid,
90 Nor no such men as you have reckoned up,
91 As Stephen Sly, and old John Naps of Greet,

---

73 *smallest* weakest   75 *wit* reason   79 *fay* faith   84 *house* inn   85 *present ... leet* accuse her before the court held by the lord of the manor (which had authority to punish such minor crimes as selling short weights and measures)   86 *brought ... quarts* i.e., brought the liquor in open stoneware pottery jugs, in which the quantity was uncertain and variable, rather than in sealed, officially certified, quart bottles   87 *Cicely Hacket* (presumably related to the alewife Marian Hacket of l. 20, and working as a maid at her inn)   90 *reckoned up* named   91 *Greet* a Gloucestershire village near Stratford

And Peter Turph, and Henry Pimpernell,
And twenty more such names and men as these,
Which never were nor no man ever saw.

SLY

Now Lord be thankèd for my good amends!   95

ALL   Amen.

Enter [the Page as a] Lady, with Attendants.

SLY   I thank thee, thou shalt not lose by it.

PAGE   How fares my noble lord?

SLY   Marry, I fare well, for here is cheer enough. Where is   99
my wife?   100

PAGE

Here, noble lord, what is thy will with her?

SLY

Are you my wife and will not call me husband?
My men should call me lord; I am your goodman.   103

PAGE

My husband and my lord, my lord and husband,
I am your wife in all obedience.

SLY   I know it well. What must I call her?

LORD   Madam.

SLY   Al'ce madam or Joan madam?

LORD

Madam and nothing else, so lords call ladies.

SLY

Madam wife, they say that I have dreamed   110
And slept above some fifteen year or more.

PAGE

Ay, and the time seems thirty unto me,
Being all this time abandoned from your bed.   113

SLY

'Tis much. Servants, leave me and her alone.

[Exeunt Lord and Servants.]

---

95 *amends* recovery   **99** *Marry* (a mild interjection, originally an oath invoking the Virgin Mary); *cheer* entertainment   **103** *goodman* husband (but the term is appropriate to a peasant, not a lord)   **113** *abandoned* banished

Madam, undress you and come now to bed.
PAGE
    Thrice-noble lord, let me entreat of you
    To pardon me yet for a night or two,
    Or if not so, until the sun be set.
    For your physicians have expressly charged,
120   In peril to incur your former malady,
    That I should yet absent me from your bed.
    I hope this reason stands for my excuse.
123 SLY Ay, it stands so that I may hardly tarry so long – but
    I would be loath to fall into my dreams again. I will
125   therefore tarry in despite of the flesh and the blood.
      Enter a Messenger.
MESSENGER
    Your honor's players, hearing your amendment,
    Are come to play a pleasant comedy,
    For so your doctors hold it very meet,
    Seeing too much sadness hath congealed your blood
130   And melancholy is the nurse of frenzy.
    Therefore they thought it good you hear a play
    And frame your mind to mirth and merriment,
    Which bars a thousand harms and lengthens life.
134 SLY Marry, I will, let them play it. Is not a commonty a
    Christmas gambol or a tumbling trick?
PAGE
    No, my good lord, it is more pleasing stuff.
SLY What, household stuff?
138 PAGE It is a kind of history.
SLY Well, we'll see't. Come, madam, wife, sit by my side
140   and let the world slip: we shall ne'er be younger.
      [They sit over the stage.]

        *

---

123 *it stands so* (1) as it happens, (2) since I have an erection **125 s.d.** *Messenger* (presumably the lord reenters as the messenger) **130** *frenzy* madness **134** *commonty* (Sly's mistake for "comedy") **138** *history* story

∾ **I.1** *Flourish. Enter [below] Lucentio and his man Tranio.*

LUCENTIO
  Tranio, since for the great desire I had
  To see fair Padua, nursery of arts,   2
  I am arrived in fruitful Lombardy,   3
  The pleasant garden of great Italy,
  And by my father's love and leave am armed
  With his good will and thy good company,
  My trusty servant, well approved in all,   7
  Here let us breathe and haply institute
  A course of learning and ingenious studies.   9
  Pisa, renownèd for grave citizens,   10
  Gave me my being and my father first,   11
  A merchant of great traffic through the world,
  Vincentio, come of the Bentivolii.
  Vincentio's son, brought up in Florence,
  It shall become to serve all hopes conceived,   15
  To deck his fortune with his virtuous deeds.
  And therefore, Tranio, for the time I study
  Virtue, and that part of philosophy
  Will I apply that treats of happiness
  By virtue specially to be achieved.   19
  Tell me thy mind, for I have Pisa left   20
  And am to Padua come, as he that leaves
  A shallow plash to plunge him in the deep   23
  And with satiety seeks to quench his thirst.
TRANIO
  Mi perdonato, gentle master mine.   25

I.1 A street in Padua   **s.d.** *man* servant; *Tranio* (name from the *Mostellaria* of Plautus connoting "clarifier, revealer")   **2** *Padua* (famous for its university)   **3** *Lombardy* northern Italy   **7** *approved* i.e., proved dependable   **9** *ingenious* intellectual   **11** *first* i.e., before me   **15** *serve . . . conceived* i.e., fulfill his father's hopes for him   **19** *apply* pursue   **23** *plash* pool   **25** *Mi perdonato* pardon me (Italian)

26 I am in all affected as yourself,
    Glad that you thus continue your resolve
    To suck the sweets of sweet philosophy.
    Only, good master, while we do admire
30 This virtue and this moral discipline,
31 Let's be no stoics nor no stocks, I pray,
32 Or so devote to Aristotle's checks
33 As Ovid be an outcast quite abjured.
34 Balk logic with acquaintance that you have
    And practice rhetoric in your common talk.
36 Music and poesy use to quicken you.
    The mathematics and the metaphysics,
38 Fall to them as you find your stomach serves you.
    No profit grows where is no pleasure ta'en.
40 In brief, sir, study what you most affect.

    LUCENTIO
41 Gramercies, Tranio, well dost thou advise.
42 If Biondello now were come ashore,
    We could at once put us in readiness
    And take a lodging fit to entertain
    Such friends as time in Padua shall beget.
    But stay awhile, what company is this?

    TRANIO
47 Master, some show to welcome us to town.
        Enter Baptista with his two daughters
        Kate and Bianca, Gremio a pantaloon,
        [and] Hortensio suitor to Bianca.
        Lucentio [and] Tranio stand by.

---

26 *affected* inclined   31 *stocks* posts (i.e., incapable of feeling; punning on *stoics*)   32 *checks* restraints   33 *As . . . abjured* i.e., that we would have to give up everything that Ovid, the Roman love poet, represents (cf. III.1.28–29; IV.2.8)   34 *Balk logic* bandy logical arguments   36 *quicken* enliven   38 *stomach* appetite   40 *affect* like   41 *Gramercies* many thanks   42 *come ashore* (like Mantua and Bergamo later, Padua is not, in fact, a seaport, though one could reach it from Venice by river and canal)   47 **s.d.** *pantaloon* foolish old man (a stock character in the commedia dell'arte)

BAPTISTA

    Gentlemen, importune me no further,
    For how I firmly am resolved you know.
    That is, not to bestow my youngest daughter   *50*
    Before I have a husband for the elder.
    If either of you both love Katherina,
    Because I know you well and love you well,
    Leave shall you have to court her at your pleasure.

GREMIO

    To cart her rather, she's too rough for me.   *55*
    There, there, Hortensio, will you any wife?

KATE

    I pray you, sir, is it your will
    To make a stale of me amongst these mates?   *58*

HORTENSIO

    "Mates," maid, how mean you that? No mates for you
    Unless you were of gentler, milder mold.   *60*

KATE

    I' faith, sir, you shall never need to fear:
    Iwis it is not halfway to her heart.   *62*
    But if it were, doubt not her care should be
    To comb your noddle with a three-legged stool
    And paint your face and use you like a fool.   *65*

HORTENSIO

    From all such devils, good Lord deliver us.

GREMIO

    And me too, good Lord.

TRANIO   *[Aside]*

    Hush, master, here's some good pastime toward.   *68*
    That wench is stark mad or wonderful froward.   *69*

---

55 *cart her* i.e., have her driven through the streets in a cart, like a prostitute undergoing punishment **58** *stale* (1) laughingstock, (2) prostitute (suggested by *cart*); *mates* (1) boors, (2) potential husbands (and the conjunction quibbles on "stalemate") **60** *mold* character **62** *Iwis* indeed; *it* i.e., marriage; *her* i.e., Kate's **65** *paint* redden (by drawing blood) **68** *toward* in prospect **69** *wonderful froward* extremely obstinate

LUCENTIO

70 But in the other's silence do I see
Maid's mild behavior and sobriety.
Peace, Tranio!

TRANIO

Well said, master; mum, and gaze your fill.

BAPTISTA

Gentlemen, that I may soon make good
What I have said – Bianca, get you in,
And let it not displease thee, good Bianca,
For I will love thee ne'er the less, my girl.

KATE

78 A pretty peat! it is best
Put finger in the eye, an she knew why.

BIANCA

80 Sister, content you in my discontent.
Sir, to your pleasure humbly I subscribe.
My books and instruments shall be my company,
On them to look and practice by myself.

LUCENTIO *[Aside]*

84 Hark, Tranio, thou mayst hear Minerva speak.

HORTENSIO

85 Signor Baptista, will you be so strange?
Sorry am I that our good will effects

87 Bianca's grief.

GREMIO   Why, will you mew her up,
Signor Baptista, for this fiend of hell
And make her bear the penance of her tongue?

BAPTISTA

90 Gentlemen, content ye, I am resolved.
Go in, Bianca.   *[Exit Bianca.]*

92 And for I know she taketh most delight

_____

78 *peat* spoiled darling 78–79 *it . . . why* if she knew what she was doing, she
would have been better off to put on a show of weeping 84 *Minerva* goddess of wisdom and of the arts 85 *strange* unnatural 87 *mew* coop (term
for caging a falcon) 92 *for* since

In music, instruments, and poetry,
Schoolmasters will I keep within my house,
Fit to instruct her youth. If you, Hortensio,
Or Signor Gremio, you, know any such,
Prefer them hither, for to cunning men   97
I will be very kind, and liberal
To mine own children in good bringing-up.
And so, farewell. Katherina, you may stay,   100
For I have more to commune with Bianca.   *Exit.*   101

KATE   Why, and I trust I may go too, may I not? What,
shall I be appointed hours, as though, belike, I knew   103
not what to take and what to leave? Ha!   *Exit.*

GREMIO   You may go to the devil's dam. Your gifts are so   105
good, here's none will hold you. Their love is not so   106
great, Hortensio, but we may blow our nails together   107
and fast it fairly out. Our cake's dough on both sides.   108
Farewell – yet for the love I bear my sweet Bianca, if I
can by any means light on a fit man to teach her that   *110*
wherein she delights, I will wish him to her father.   111

HORTENSIO   So will I, Signor Gremio. But a word, I
pray. Though the nature of our quarrel yet never
brooked parley, know now, upon advice it toucheth us   114
both, that we may yet again have access to our fair mistress and be happy rivals in Bianca's love, to labor and
effect one thing specially.

GREMIO   What's that, I pray?

HORTENSIO   Marry, sir, to get a husband for her sister.

GREMIO   A husband? A devil.   *120*

HORTENSIO   I say, a husband.

GREMIO   I say, a devil. Think'st thou, Hortensio, though
her father be very rich, any man is so very a fool to be   123
married to hell?

---

97 *Prefer* recommend; *cunning* well-trained **101** *commune* discuss **103** *belike* presumably **105** *dam* mother **106** *hold* endure; *Their* i.e., women's
107 *blow . . . together* i.e., be patient **108** *Our cake's dough* i.e., our expecta-
tions are disappointed (proverbial) **111** *wish* recommend **114** *brooked
parley* permitted discussion; *advice* reflection **123** *so very a* such a complete

HORTENSIO Tush, Gremio, though it pass your patience
126 and mine to endure her loud alarums, why, man, there
127 be good fellows in the world, an a man could light on
them, would take her with all her faults, and money
enough.
130 GREMIO I cannot tell, but I had as lief take her dowry
131 with this condition, to be whipped at the high cross
every morning.
HORTENSIO Faith, as you say, there's small choice in rot-
134 ten apples. But come, since this bar in law makes us
friends, it shall be so far forth friendly maintained, till
by helping Baptista's eldest daughter to a husband we
137 set his youngest free for a husband, and then have to't
138 afresh. Sweet Bianca! Happy man be his dole. He that
139 runs fastest gets the ring. How say you, Signor Gremio?
140 GREMIO I am agreed, and would I had given him the
best horse in Padua to begin his wooing that would
thoroughly woo her, wed her, and bed her, and rid the
143 house of her. Come on.
                    Exeunt ambo. Manent Tranio and Lucentio.
TRANIO
   I pray, sir, tell me, is it possible
   That love should of a sudden take such hold?
LUCENTIO
   O Tranio, till I found it to be true
   I never thought it possible or likely.
   But see, while idly I stood looking on,
149 I found the effect of love-in-idleness
150 And now in plainness do confess to thee,
   That art to me as secret and as dear
152 As Anna to the Queen of Carthage was,

---

126 *alarums* calls to arms 127 *an* if 131 *high cross* market cross (i.e., the center of town) 134 *bar* obstacle 137 *have to't* let us set to it 138 *Happy . . . dole* happiness be his lot (i.e., his who wins her; proverbial) 139 *ring* prize (playing on "wedding ring") 143 s.d. *ambo* both (Gremio and Hortensio); *Manent* remain 149 *love-in-idleness* the pansy (supposed to have magical power in love) 152 *Anna* Dido's sister and confidante

Tranio, I burn, I pine, I perish, Tranio,
If I achieve not this young modest girl.   154
Counsel me, Tranio, for I know thou canst.
Assist me, Tranio, for I know thou wilt.

TRANIO

Master, it is no time to chide you now.
Affection is not rated from the heart.   158
If love have touched you, nought remains but so,
"Redime te captum, quam queas minimo."   160

LUCENTIO

Gramercies, lad. Go forward, this contents;
The rest will comfort, for thy counsel's sound.

TRANIO

Master, you looked so longly on the maid,   163
Perhaps you marked not what's the pith of all.

LUCENTIO

O yes, I saw sweet beauty in her face,
Such as the daughter of Agenor had,   166
That made great Jove to humble him to her hand
When with his knees he kissed the Cretan strand.

TRANIO

Saw you no more? Marked you not how her sister
Began to scold and raise up such a storm   *170*
That mortal ears might hardly endure the din?

LUCENTIO

Tranio, I saw her coral lips to move,   172
And with her breath she did perfume the air.   173
Sacred and sweet was all I saw in her.

TRANIO

Nay, then, 'tis time to stir him from his trance.
I pray, awake, sir. If you love the maid

_____

154 *achieve* win   158 *rated* driven out by scolding   160 *Redime . . . minimo*
redeem yourself from captivity as cheaply as you can (from the *Eunuchus* of
Terence but quoted from Lily's *Latin Grammar*)   163 *longly* longingly   166
daughter of Agenor Europa (loved by Jupiter, who in the shape of a bull ab-
ducted her)   172, 173 *coral, perfume* (hackneyed comparisons of the Petrar-
chan sonnet tradition; cf. Shakespeare's Sonnet 130)

Bend thoughts and wits to achieve her. Thus it stands:

178   Her elder sister is so curst and shrewd

That till the father rid his hands of her,

180   Master, your love must live a maid at home,

181   And therefore has he closely mewed her up,

182   Because she will not be annoyed with suitors.

LUCENTIO

Ah, Tranio, what a cruel father's he.

184   But art thou not advised he took some care

To get her cunning schoolmasters to instruct her?

TRANIO

186   Ay, marry, am I, sir, and now 'tis plotted.

LUCENTIO

187   I have it, Tranio.

TRANIO   Master, for my hand,

188   Both our inventions meet and jump in one.

LUCENTIO

Tell me thine first.

TRANIO   You will be schoolmaster

190   And undertake the teaching of the maid.

That's your device.

LUCENTIO   It is. May it be done?

TRANIO

Not possible, for who shall bear your part

And be in Padua here Vincentio's son,

Keep house and ply his book, welcome his friends,

Visit his countrymen and banquet them?

LUCENTIO

196   Basta, content thee, for I have it full.

We have not yet been seen in any house

Nor can we be distinguished by our faces

For man or master. Then it follows thus.

---

178 *curst* bad-tempered; *shrewd* shrewish   181 *mewed* cooped   182 *Because*
so that   184 *advised* aware   186 *'tis plotted* I have a plan   187 *for . . . hand*
I'll wager   188 *inventions* plans; *jump* agree   196 *Basta* enough; *have it full*
see it clearly

Thou shalt be master, Tranio, in my stead,   200
Keep house and port and servants as I should.   201
I will some other be, some Florentine,
Some Neapolitan or meaner man of Pisa.
'Tis hatched and shall be so. Tranio, at once   203
Uncase thee, take my colored hat and cloak.   205
When Biondello comes he waits on thee,
But I will charm him first to keep his tongue.

TRANIO
So had you need.
    [They exchange cloaks and hats.]
In brief, sir, sith it your pleasure is   209
And I am tied to be obedient –   210
For so your father charged me at our parting,
"Be serviceable to my son," quoth he,
Although I think 'twas in another sense –
I am content to be Lucentio
Because so well I love Lucentio.

LUCENTIO
Tranio, be so, because Lucentio loves,
And let me be a slave, t' achieve that maid
Whose sudden sight hath thralled my wounded eye.   218
    Enter Biondello.
Here comes the rogue. – Sirrah, where have you been?   219

BIONDELLO
Where have I been? Nay, how now, where are you?   220
Master, has my fellow Tranio stol'n your clothes,
Or you stol'n his, or both? Pray, what's the news?

LUCENTIO
Sirrah, come hither. 'Tis no time to jest,
And therefore frame your manners to the time.
Your fellow Tranio, here, to save my life,
Puts my apparel and my count'nance on,   226

---

201 *port* style of living 203 *meaner* i.e., of lower than my true rank 205
Uncase uncloak 209 *sith* since 218 *thralled* enslaved 219 *Sirrah* (usual
form of address to an inferior) 226 *count'nance* appearance, deportment

And I for my escape have put on his,
For in a quarrel since I came ashore
I killed a man and fear I was descried.
230 Wait you on him, I charge you, as becomes,
While I make way from hence to save my life.
You understand me?

BIONDELLO   I, sir? Ne'er a whit.

LUCENTIO
And not a jot of Tranio in your mouth.
Tranio is changed into Lucentio.

BIONDELLO
The better for him, would I were so too.

TRANIO
So could I, faith, boy, to have the next wish after,
That Lucentio indeed had Baptista's youngest daughter.
But, sirrah, not for my sake but your master's, I advise
You use your manners discreetly in all kind of compa-
    nies.
240 When I am alone, why then I am Tranio,
But in all places else, your master Lucentio.

LUCENTIO
Tranio, let's go.
243 One thing more rests, that thyself execute –
To make one among these wooers. If thou ask me why,
245 Sufficeth my reasons are both good and weighty.

                                            Exeunt.

    The Presenters above speak.

246 FIRST SERVINGMAN   My lord, you nod, you do not mind
    the play.

SLY   Yes, by Saint Anne, do I. A good matter, surely.
    Comes there any more of it?

250 PAGE   My lord, 'tis but begun.

---

243 *rests* remains; *execute* arrange   245 s.d. *Presenters* choral characters of an
induction who "present" the play proper   246 *mind* pay attention to

SLY   'Tis a very excellent piece of work, madam lady –
   would 'twere done.   252
   They sit and mark.

✳

❧ **I.2** *Enter [below] Petruchio and his man Grumio.*

PETRUCHIO
  Verona, for awhile I take my leave
  To see my friends in Padua, but of all
  My best belovèd and approvèd friend
  Hortensio; and I trow this is his house.   4
  Here, sirrah Grumio, knock, I say.
GRUMIO   Knock, sir? Whom should I knock? Is there
  any man has rebused your worship?   7
PETRUCHIO   Villain, I say, knock me here soundly.   8
GRUMIO   Knock you here, sir? Why, sir, what am I, sir,
  that I should knock you here, sir?   10
PETRUCHIO
  Villain, I say, knock me at this gate,   11
  And rap me well or I'll knock your knave's pate.
GRUMIO
  My master is grown quarrelsome. I should knock you
    first,
  And then I know after who comes by the worst.
PETRUCHIO
  Will it not be?
  Faith, sirrah, an you'll not knock, I'll ring it.   16

---

252 s.d. *They sit and mark* (the presenters are not heard from again; see the
Introduction); *mark* watch
  I.2 A street in Padua **s.d.** *Petruchio* (Shakespeare's phonetic spelling of
Petruccio, diminutive of Pietro; pronounced "Petrutchio," not "Petruckio");
Grumio (the name, like Tranio, is that of a slave in Plautus's *Mostellaria*)
4 *trow* believe **7** *rebused* (Grumio's mistake for "abused") **8** *me* i.e., for me
(but Grumio, perhaps deliberately, misunderstands) **11** *gate* door **16** *ring*
(playing on "wring")

17   I'll try how you can sol, fa, and sing it.
         He wrings him by the ears.

GRUMIO
18   Help, masters, help! My master is mad.

PETRUCHIO
      Now, knock when I bid you, sirrah villain.
         Enter Hortensio.

20 HORTENSIO   How now, what's the matter? My old friend
      Grumio, and my good friend Petruchio! How do you
      all at Verona?

PETRUCHIO
      Signor Hortensio, come you to part the fray?
24   *Con tutto il cuore bentrovato,* may I say.

HORTENSIO
25   *Alla nostra casa benvenuto,*
      Molto honorato signor mio Petruchio.
27   Rise, Grumio, rise, we will compound this quarrel.

28 GRUMIO   Nay, 'tis no matter, sir, what he 'leges in Latin.
      If this be not a lawful cause for me to leave his service,
30   look you, sir; he bid me knock him and rap him
      soundly, sir. Well, was it fit for a servant to use his mas-
32   ter so, being perhaps, for aught I see, two and thirty, a
      pip out?
      Whom would to God I had well knocked at first,
      Then had not Grumio come by the worst.

PETRUCHIO
      A senseless villain. Good Hortensio,
      I bade the rascal knock upon your gate
      And could not get him for my heart to do it.

---

17 *sol, fa* sing the scale 18 *Help, masters* (to the audience) 24 *Con . . . trovato* with all my heart well met (Italian) 25–26 *Alla . . . Petruchio* welcome to our house, my very honorable Signor Petruchio (Italian) 27 *compound* settle 28 *'leges* alleges 32–33 *two . . . out* very drunk (a slang expression derived from the card game one-and-thirty, hence a little more drunk than drunk; a *pip* is the mark identifying the suit on a playing card, such as a heart or spade)

GRUMIO   Knock at the gate? O heavens! Spake you not
these words plain, "Sirrah, knock me here, rap me here,   40
knock me well, and knock me soundly"? And come you
now with "knocking at the gate"?

PETRUCHIO
Sirrah, be gone, or talk not, I advise you.

HORTENSIO
Petruchio, patience, I am Grumio's pledge.
Why, this' a heavy chance 'twixt him and you,   45
Your ancient, trusty, pleasant servant Grumio.
And tell me now, sweet friend, what happy gale
Blows you to Padua here from old Verona?

PETRUCHIO
Such wind as scatters young men through the world
To seek their fortunes farther than at home,   50
Where small experience grows. But in a few,   51
Signor Hortensio, thus it stands with me.
Antonio my father is deceased,
And I have thrust myself into this maze,
Happily to wive and thrive as best I may.   55
Crowns in my purse I have and goods at home,
And so am come abroad to see the world.

HORTENSIO
Petruchio, shall I then come roundly to thee   58
And wish thee to a shrewd ill-favored wife?   59
Thou'dst thank me but a little for my counsel.   60
And yet I'll promise thee she shall be rich,
And very rich – but thou'rt too much my friend
And I'll not wish thee to her.

PETRUCHIO
Signor Hortensio, 'twixt such friends as we
Few words suffice. And therefore if thou know
One rich enough to be Petruchio's wife –

---

45 *this'* this is; *heavy chance* sad event   51 *in a few* i.e., words   55 *Happily*
(1) cheerfully, (2) by chance   58 *come roundly* speak plainly   59 *shrewd*
shrewish; *ill-favored* ill-natured

67 As wealth is burden of my wooing dance –
68 Be she as foul as was Florentius' love,
69 As old as Sibyl, and as curst and shrewd
70 As Socrates' Xanthippe, or a worse,
   She moves me not, or not removes, at least,
   Affection's edge in me, were she as rough
   As are the swelling Adriatic seas.
   I come to wive it wealthily in Padua –
   If wealthily, then happily in Padua.

GRUMIO   Nay, look you, sir, he tells you flatly what his
   mind is. Why, give him gold enough and marry him to
78 a puppet or an aglet-baby or an old trot with ne'er a
   tooth in her head, though she have as many diseases as
80 two and fifty horses. Why, nothing comes amiss, so
81 money comes withal.

HORTENSIO
   Petruchio, since we are stepped thus far in,
83 I will continue that I broached in jest.
   I can, Petruchio, help thee to a wife
   With wealth enough, and young and beauteous,
   Brought up as best becomes a gentlewoman.
   Her only fault – and that is faults enough –
   Is that she is intolerable curst,
89 And shrewd and froward, so beyond all measure,
90 That were my state far worser than it is
   I would not wed her for a mine of gold.

PETRUCHIO
   Hortensio, peace. Thou know'st not gold's effect.

---

67 *burden* bass or undersong 68 *foul* ugly; *Florentius* (A knight who married an old hag in return for the answer to a riddle – "What do women most desire?" – that would save his life; the answer is to rule their husbands. She then turned into a beautiful maiden; cf. Gower's *Confessio Amantis*, Book I, or Chaucer's Wife of Bath's Tale.) 69 *Sibyl* the Cumaean Sibyl (a prophetess to whom Apollo granted as many years of life as she could hold grains of sand in her hand) 70 *Xanthippe* (the philosopher's wife, reputedly a shrew) 78 *aglet-baby* tiny doll figure (aglet indicating either a spangle or the metal "point" of a lace); *trot* hag 81 *withal* at the same time 83 *that* that which 89 *froward* obstinate

Tell me her father's name, and 'tis enough,
For I will board her though she chide as loud   94
As thunder when the clouds in autumn crack.

HORTENSIO

Her father is Baptista Minola,
An affable and courteous gentleman.
Her name is Katherina Minola,
Renowned in Padua for her scolding tongue.

PETRUCHIO

I know her father though I know not her,
And he knew my deceasèd father well.   100
I will not sleep, Hortensio, till I see her,
And therefore let me be thus bold with you,
To give you over at this first encounter
Unless you will accompany me thither.   104

GRUMIO   I pray you, sir, let him go while the humor   106
lasts. A my word, an she knew him as well as I do, she   107
would think scolding would do little good upon him.
She may perhaps call him half a score knaves or so —
why, that's nothing, an he begin once, he'll rail in his 110
rope tricks. I'll tell you what, sir, an she stand him but a 111
little, he will throw a figure in her face and so disfigure 112
her with it that she shall have no more eyes to see
withal than a cat. You know him not, sir.

HORTENSIO

Tarry, Petruchio, I must go with thee,
For in Baptista's keep my treasure is.
He hath the jewel of my life in hold,   116
His youngest daughter, beautiful Bianca,   117
And her withholds from me and other more,
Suitors to her and rivals in my love,
Supposing it a thing impossible,   120

---

94 *board* (as in attacking a ship)   **104** *give you over* leave you   **106** *humor*
whim   **107** *A* on, by   **111** *rope tricks* (Grumio's mistake for "rhetoric" – i.e.,
abusive language, with a glance at tricks punishable by hanging); *stand* withstand   **112** *figure* rhetorical figure (i.e., a telling expression)   **116** *keep* (1)
keeping, (2) fortified tower   **117** *hold* confinement

For those defects I have before rehearsed,
That ever Katherina will be wooed.
124   Therefore this order hath Baptista ta'en,
That none shall have access unto Bianca
Till Katherine the curst have got a husband.

GRUMIO
Katherine the curst!
A title for a maid of all titles the worst.

HORTENSIO
129   Now shall my friend Petruchio do me grace
130   And offer me, disguised in sober robes,
To old Baptista as a schoolmaster
132   Well seen in music, to instruct Bianca,
That so I may, by this device, at last
Have leave and leisure to make love to her
And unsuspected court her by herself.

*Enter Gremio [with a paper] and Lucentio disguised
[as a schoolmaster].*

GRUMIO   Here's no knavery! See, to beguile the old folks,
how the young folks lay their heads together! Master,
master, look about you. Who goes there, ha?

HORTENSIO
Peace, Grumio, it is the rival of my love.
140   Petruchio, stand by awhile.

GRUMIO
141   A proper stripling, and an amorous!
[They stand aside.]

GREMIO
142   O very well, I have perused the note.
Hark you, sir, I'll have them very fairly bound,
144   All books of love, see that at any hand,
145   And see you read no other lectures to her.

---

124 *order* measure   129 *grace* a favor   132 *seen* versed   141 *proper stripling*
handsome youth (ironically, of the "pantaloon" Gremio)   142 *note* i.e., a
list of books for Bianca   144 *at any hand* in any case   145 *read* teach; *lectures* lessons

You understand me. Over and beside
Signor Baptista's liberality,
I'll mend it with a largess. Take your paper too,   148
And let me have them very well perfumed,   149
For she is sweeter than perfume itself   150
To whom they go. What will you read to her?

LUCENTIO
Whate'er I read to her, I'll plead for you,
As for my patron, stand you so assured,
As firmly as yourself were still in place,   154
Yea and perhaps with more successful words
Than you – unless you were a scholar, sir.

GREMIO
O this learning, what a thing it is!

GRUMIO   [Aside]
O this woodcock, what an ass it is!   158

PETRUCHIO
Peace, sirrah.

HORTENSIO
Grumio, mum! [Advancing] God save you, Signor   160
Gremio.

GREMIO
And you are well met, Signor Hortensio.
Trow you whither I am going? To Baptista Minola.   162
I promised to inquire carefully
About a schoolmaster for the fair Bianca,
And by good fortune I have lighted well
On this young man, for learning and behavior
Fit for her turn, well read in poetry   167
And other books, good ones, I warrant ye.

HORTENSIO
'Tis well, and I have met a gentleman
Hath promised me to help me to another,   170

---

148 *mend* increase; *largess* gift of money; *paper* i.e., the *note*   149 *them* i.e.,
the books   154 *in place* present   158 *woodcock* (bird easily caught, hence
proverbially stupid)   162 *Trow* know   167 *turn* need

171   A fine musician to instruct our mistress.
    So shall I no whit be behind in duty
    To fair Bianca, so beloved of me.

GREMIO
    Beloved of me, and that my deeds shall prove.

GRUMIO   *[Aside]*
175   And that his bags shall prove.

HORTENSIO
176   Gremio, 'tis now no time to vent our love.
    Listen to me, and if you speak me fair
178   I'll tell you news indifferent good for either.
    Here is a gentleman whom by chance I met,
180   Upon agreement from us to his liking,
181   Will undertake to woo curst Katherine,
    Yea and to marry her if her dowry please.

GREMIO
    So said, so done, is well.
    Hortensio, have you told him all her faults?

PETRUCHIO
    I know she is an irksome brawling scold.
    If that be all, masters, I hear no harm.

GREMIO
    No, sayst me so, friend? What countryman?

PETRUCHIO
    Born in Verona, old Antonio's son.
    My father dead, my fortune lives for me,
190   And I do hope good days and long to see.

GREMIO
    O sir, such a life, with such a wife, were strange.
192   But if you have a stomach, to't a God's name,
    You shall have me assisting you in all.
194   But will you woo this wildcat?

PETRUCHIO   Will I live?

---

171 *mistress* beloved   175 *bags* moneybags   176 *vent* utter   178 *indifferent* equally   180 *agreement* terms (they will pay his expenses of wooing, l. 213)   181 *Will undertake* i.e., who, upon agreement, will undertake   192 *stomach* appetite; *a* in   194 *Will I live?* i.e., certainly

GRUMIO   *[Aside]*
  Will he woo her? Ay, or he'll hang her.
PETRUCHIO
  Why came I hither but to that intent?
  Think you a little din can daunt mine ears?
  Have I not in my time heard lions roar?
  Have I not heard the sea, puffed up with winds,
  Rage like an angry boar chafèd with sweat?   200
  Have I not heard great ordnance in the field
  And heaven's artillery thunder in the skies?
  Have I not in a pitchèd battle heard
  Loud 'larums, neighing steeds, and trumpets' clang?   204
  And do you tell me of a woman's tongue,
  That gives not half so great a blow to th' ear
  As will a chestnut in a farmer's fire?
  Tush, tush, fear boys with bugs.   208
GRUMIO   *[Aside]*   For he fears none.
GREMIO
  Hortensio, hark.
  This gentleman is happily arrived,   210
  My mind presumes, for his own good and ours.
HORTENSIO
  I promised we would be contributors,
  And bear his charge of wooing whatsoe'er.   213
GREMIO
  And so we will, provided that he win her.
GRUMIO   *[Aside]*
  I would I were as sure of a good dinner.   215
    Enter Tranio brave [as Lucentio], and Biondello.
TRANIO
  Gentlemen, God save you. If I may be bold,
  Tell me, I beseech you, which is the readiest way
  To the house of Signor Baptista Minola?

---

204 *'larums* calls to arms   208 *fear* frighten; *bugs* bogeymen   213 *charge* expenses   215 s.d. *brave* finely dressed

BIONDELLO   He that has the two fair daughters, is't he
220   you mean?

TRANIO   Even he, Biondello.

GREMIO
Hark you, sir; you mean not her to woo?

TRANIO
223   Perhaps him and her, sir, what have you to do?

PETRUCHIO
Not her that chides, sir, at any hand, I pray.

TRANIO
I love no chiders, sir. – Biondello, let's away.

LUCENTIO   *[Aside]*
Well begun, Tranio.

HORTENSIO   Sir, a word ere you go.
Are you a suitor to the maid you talk of, yea or no?

TRANIO
An if I be, sir, is it any offense?

GREMIO
No, if without more words you will get you hence.

TRANIO
230   Why, sir, I pray, are not the streets as free
For me as for you?

GREMIO   But so is not she.

TRANIO
For what reason, I beseech you?

GREMIO   For this reason, if you'll
know,
That she's the choice love of Signor Gremio.

HORTENSIO
That she's the chosen of Signor Hortensio.

TRANIO
Softly, my masters. If you be gentlemen,
Do me this right, hear me with patience.
Baptista is a noble gentleman,
To whom my father is not all unknown,

---

223 *what . . . do* what business is it of yours

And were his daughter fairer than she is
She may more suitors have, and me for one.   240
Fair Leda's daughter had a thousand wooers,   241
Then well one more may fair Bianca have.   242
And so she shall: Lucentio shall make one,
Though Paris came in hope to speed alone.   244

GREMIO
What, this gentleman will outtalk us all.

LUCENTIO
Sir, give him head. I know he'll prove a jade.   246

PETRUCHIO
Hortensio, to what end are all these words?

HORTENSIO
Sir, let me be so bold as to ask you,
Did you yet ever see Baptista's daughter?

TRANIO
No, sir, but I do hear that he hath two,   250
The one as famous for a scolding tongue
As is the other for beauteous modesty.

PETRUCHIO
Sir, sir, the first's for me, let her go by.

GREMIO
Yea, leave that labor to great Hercules,
And let it be more than Alcides' twelve.   255

PETRUCHIO
Sir, understand you this of me, in sooth.   256
The youngest daughter, whom you hearken for,   257
Her father keeps from all access of suitors
And will not promise her to any man
Until the elder sister first be wed.   260

---

241 *Leda's daughter* Helen of Troy (Leda was made love to by Jupiter in the shape of a swan)   242 *one more* i.e., than she now has   244 *Paris* Helen's lover (who took her away from her husband, Menelaus); *came* were to come; *speed* succeed   246 *jade* worthless horse (easily tired)   255 *Alcides* Hercules (so called from his grandfather Alcaeus); *twelve* (Hercules was required to perform twelve labors, or impossible tasks)   256 *sooth* truth   257 *hearken for* ask after

The younger then is free, and not before.

TRANIO
If it be so, sir, that you are the man
263   Must stead us all, and me amongst the rest,
And if you break the ice and do this feat,
265   Achieve the elder, set the younger free
266   For our access, whose hap shall be to have her
Will not so graceless be to be ingrate.

HORTENSIO
268   Sir, you say well, and well you do conceive,
And since you do profess to be a suitor,
270   You must, as we do, gratify this gentleman,
271   To whom we all rest generally beholding.

TRANIO
Sir, I shall not be slack, in sign whereof,
273   Please ye we may contrive this afternoon
274   And quaff carouses to our mistress' health,
275   And do as adversaries do in law,
Strive mightily but eat and drink as friends.

GRUMIO, BIONDELLO
O excellent motion! Fellows, let's be gone.

HORTENSIO
The motion's good indeed, and be it so.
279   Petruchio, I shall be your *benvenuto*.   *Exeunt.*

                              ✳

❧ **II.1** *Enter Kate and Bianca [with her hands tied].*

BIANCA
Good sister, wrong me not, nor wrong yourself,
To make a bondmaid and a slave of me –

---

263 *stead* help   **265** *Achieve* win   **266** *whose hap* he whose luck   **268** *well you . . . conceive* you understand the matter well   **270** *gratify* reward   **271** *beholding* beholden, indebted   **273** *contrive* pass the time   **274** *quaff carouses* drink toasts   **275** *adversaries* lawyers (not their clients)   **279** *benvenuto* welcome (Italian)
  II.1 Baptista's house

That I disdain. But for these other gawds,   3
Unbind my hands, I'll pull them off myself,
Yea, all my raiment, to my petticoat,
Or what you will command me will I do,
So well I know my duty to my elders.

KATE
Of all thy suitors, here I charge thee, tell
Whom thou lov'st best. See thou dissemble not.

BIANCA
Believe me, sister, of all the men alive
I never yet beheld that special face   10
Which I could fancy more than any other.

KATE
Minion, thou liest. Is't not Hortensio?   13

BIANCA
If you affect him, sister, here I swear   14
I'll plead for you myself but you shall have him.

KATE
O then, belike, you fancy riches more.
You will have Gremio to keep you fair.   16
                                                                     17

BIANCA
Is it for him you do envy me so?
Nay, then you jest, and now I well perceive   18
You have but jested with me all this while.
I prithee, sister Kate, untie my hands.   20

KATE
If that be jest then all the rest was so.
    Strikes her.
    Enter Baptista.

BAPTISTA
Why, how now, dame, whence grows this insolence?
Bianca, stand aside. Poor girl, she weeps.
Go ply thy needle, meddle not with her.
For shame, thou hilding of a devilish spirit,   26

---

3 *gawds* ornaments 13 *Minion* minx 14 *affect* love 16 *belike* probably
17 *fair* in finery 18 *envy* hate 26 *hilding* vicious beast

Why dost thou wrong her that did ne'er wrong thee?
When did she cross thee with a bitter word?

KATE
Her silence flouts me and I'll be revenged.
Flies after Bianca.

BAPTISTA
30   What, in my sight? Bianca, get thee in.   *Exit [Bianca].*

KATE
Will you not suffer me? Nay, now I see
She is your treasure, she must have a husband;
33   I must dance barefoot on her wedding day,
34   And for your love to her lead apes in hell.
Talk not to me, I will go sit and weep
Till I can find occasion of revenge.   *[Exit.]*

BAPTISTA
Was ever gentleman thus grieved as I?
38   But who comes here?
*Enter Gremio, [with] Lucentio [as a schoolmaster] in
the habit of a mean man, Petruchio with [Hortensio as
a music master, and] Tranio [as Lucentio] with his boy
[Biondello] bearing a lute and books.*

GREMIO   Good morrow, neighbor Baptista.

40 BAPTISTA   Good morrow, neighbor Gremio. God save
you, gentlemen.

PETRUCHIO
And you, good sir. Pray, have you not a daughter
Called Katherina, fair and virtuous?

BAPTISTA
I have a daughter, sir, called Katherina.

GREMIO
45   You are too blunt, go to it orderly.

---

33 *dance . . . day* (proverbially the fate of an unmarried elder sister) 34
lead . . . hell (proverbial fate of old maids) 38 s.d. *habit* garments; *mean*
lower-class; *boy* page 45 *orderly* politely

PETRUCHIO
 You wrong me, Signor Gremio, give me leave.
 I am a gentleman of Verona, sir,
 That, hearing of her beauty and her wit,
 Her affability and bashful modesty,
 Her wondrous qualities and mild behavior,   *50*
 Am bold to show myself a forward guest
 Within your house, to make mine eye the witness
 Of that report which I so oft have heard.
 And for an entrance to my entertainment
 I do present you with a man of mine,   *54*
  [Presenting Hortensio]
 Cunning in music and the mathematics,
 To instruct her fully in those sciences,
 Whereof I know she is not ignorant.
 Accept of him or else you do me wrong.
 His name is Litio, born in Mantua.   *60*
BAPTISTA
 You're welcome, sir, and he for your good sake.
 But for my daughter Katherine, this I know,
 She is not for your turn, the more my grief.   *63*
PETRUCHIO
 I see you do not mean to part with her,
 Or else you like not of my company.
BAPTISTA
 Mistake me not, I speak but as I find.
 Whence are you, sir? What may I call your name?
PETRUCHIO
 Petruchio is my name, Antonio's son,
 A man well known throughout all Italy.
BAPTISTA
 I know him well, you are welcome for his sake.   *70*

---

54 *entrance* entrance fee; *entertainment* welcome (as a suitor) **60** *Litio* (or
Lizio, an old Italian word for garlic; pronounced "Leet-sio") **63** *turn* purpose **70** *know him* i.e., know who he is

71 GREMIO   Saving your tale, Petruchio, I pray, let us, that
72   are poor petitioners, speak too. Backare, you are mar-
      velous forward.

PETRUCHIO

74   O pardon me, Signor Gremio, I would fain be doing.

      GREMIO   I doubt it not, sir, but you will curse your woo-
      ing. Neighbor, this is a gift very grateful, I am sure of it.
      To express the like kindness, myself, that have been
      more kindly beholding to you than any, freely give
      unto you this young scholar, *[Presenting Lucentio]* that
80   hath been long studying at Rheims; as cunning in
      Greek, Latin, and other languages as the other in music
82   and mathematics. His name is Cambio, pray accept his
      service.

      BAPTISTA   A thousand thanks, Signor Gremio. Welcome,
      good Cambio. *[To Tranio]* But, gentle sir, methinks you
      walk like a stranger. May I be so bold to know the cause
      of your coming?

TRANIO

      Pardon me, sir, the boldness is mine own,
      That, being a stranger in this city here,
90   Do make myself a suitor to your daughter,
      Unto Bianca, fair and virtuous.
      Nor is your firm resolve unknown to me
      In the preferment of the eldest sister.
      This liberty is all that I request,
      That, upon knowledge of my parentage,
      I may have welcome 'mongst the rest that woo,
      And free access and favor as the rest.
      And toward the education of your daughters
      I here bestow a simple instrument,
100   And this small packet of Greek and Latin books.
      If you accept them, then their worth is great.

---

71 *Saving* with no disrespect to   72 *Backare* back off (pronounced "back-
AR-ay"; mock Latin)   74 *fain* gladly   80 *Rheims* (here pronounced "reams")
82 *Cambio* (the word means "exchange" in Italian)

BAPTISTA

Lucentio is your name, of whence, I pray?   102

TRANIO

Of Pisa, sir, son to Vincentio.

BAPTISTA

A mighty man of Pisa by report,

I know him well. You are very welcome, sir.   105

   [To Hortensio]

Take you the lute, *[To Lucentio]* and you the set of
   books.

You shall go see your pupils presently.   107

Holla, within!

   Enter a Servant.

Sirrah, lead these gentlemen

To my daughters, and tell them both   110

These are their tutors; bid them use them well.

                 [Exit Servant with Hortensio,
                    Lucentio, and Biondello.]

We will go walk a little in the orchard   112

And then to dinner. You are passing welcome,   113

And so I pray you all to think yourselves.

PETRUCHIO

Signor Baptista, my business asketh haste,

And every day I cannot come to woo.

You knew my father well, and in him me,

Left solely heir to all his lands and goods,

Which I have bettered rather than decreased.

Then tell me, if I get your daughter's love   120

What dowry shall I have with her to wife?

BAPTISTA

After my death the one half of my lands,

And in possession twenty thousand crowns.   123

---

102 *Lucentio* (Tranio has not mentioned the name yet: does he offer Baptista
some identification? Does Baptista find his name in one of the books?)   **105**
know him i.e., know who he is   **107** *presently* immediately   **112** *orchard* garden   **113** *dinner* (the main meal, served at midday); *passing* exceedingly
123 *possession* i.e., immediate possession

PETRUCHIO
   And for that dowry, I'll assure her of
125   Her widowhood, be it that she survive me,
   In all my lands and leases whatsoever.
127   Let specialties be therefore drawn between us,
   That covenants may be kept on either hand.
BAPTISTA
   Ay, when the special thing is well obtained,
130   That is, her love, for that is all in all.
PETRUCHIO
   Why, that is nothing, for I tell you, father,
132   I am as peremptory as she proud-minded,
   And where two raging fires meet together
   They do consume the thing that feeds their fury.
   Though little fire grows great with little wind,
   Yet extreme gusts will blow out fire and all.
   So I to her, and so she yields to me,
   For I am rough and woo not like a babe.
BAPTISTA
139   Well mayst thou woo, and happy be thy speed,
140   But be thou armed for some unhappy words.
PETRUCHIO
141   Ay, to the proof, as mountains are for winds,
142   That shakes not though they blow perpetually.
      Enter Hortensio [as Litio] with his head broke.
BAPTISTA
   How now, my friend, why dost thou look so pale?
HORTENSIO
   For fear, I promise you, if I look pale.
BAPTISTA
   What, will my daughter prove a good musician?
HORTENSIO
   I think she'll sooner prove a soldier.

----

125 *widowhood* income if widowed   127 *specialties* contracts   132 *peremptory* determined   139 *speed* fortune   141 *to the proof* in tested armor   142
s.d. *broke* i.e., with the skin broken, bleeding

Iron may hold with her but never lutes.   147

BAPTISTA

Why, then thou canst not break her to the lute?   148

HORTENSIO

Why, no, for she hath broke the lute to me.
I did but tell her she mistook her frets   150
And bowed her hand to teach her fingering,   151
When, with a most impatient devilish spirit,
"Frets, call you these?" quoth she, "I'll fume with them."
And with that word she struck me on the head,
And through the instrument my pate made way,
And there I stood amazèd for a while
As on a pillory, looking through the lute,
While she did call me rascal, fiddler,
And twangling Jack, with twenty such vile terms,   159
As had she studied to misuse me so.

PETRUCHIO   160

Now, by the world, it is a lusty wench.
I love her ten times more than e'er I did.   161
O how I long to have some chat with her!

BAPTISTA   *[To Hortensio]*

Well, go with me, and be not so discomfited.
Proceed in practice with my younger daughter.
She's apt to learn and thankful for good turns.
Signor Petruchio, will you go with us   166
Or shall I send my daughter Kate to you?

PETRUCHIO

I pray you do. I will attend her here,   169

*Exit [Baptista with Gremio, Tranio,
and Hortensio]. Manet Petruchio.*

And woo her with some spirit when she comes.
Say that she rail, why then I'll tell her plain   170

---

147 *hold with her* (1) suit her, (2) withstand her; *lutes* (playing on "cement
made of clay") 148 *break* tame 150 *frets* rings of gut, placed on the finger-
board to regulate the fingering (Kate quibbled on "fret and fume," be indig-
nant) 151 *bowed* bent 159 *Jack* knave 161 *lusty* lively 166 *apt* willing
169 *attend* wait for

She sings as sweetly as a nightingale.
Say that she frown, I'll say she looks as clear
As morning roses newly washed with dew.
Say she be mute and will not speak a word,
Then I'll commend her volubility
And say she uttereth piercing eloquence.
If she do bid me pack I'll give her thanks
As though she bid me stay by her a week.
180 If she deny to wed I'll crave the day
181 When I shall ask the banns, and when be marrièd.
    Enter Kate.
But here she comes, and now, Petruchio, speak.
Good morrow, Kate, for that's your name, I hear.

KATE
184 Well have you heard, but something hard of hearing.
They call me Katherine that do talk of me.

PETRUCHIO
You lie, in faith, for you are called plain Kate,
187 And bonny Kate, and sometimes Kate the curst.
But Kate, the prettiest Kate in Christendom,
Kate of Kate Hall, my superdainty Kate,
190 For dainties are all cates, and therefore, Kate,
Take this of me, Kate of my consolation:
Hearing thy mildness praised in every town,
193 Thy virtues spoke of, and thy beauty sounded,
Yet not so deeply as to thee belongs,
Myself am moved to woo thee for my wife.

KATE
196 Moved? In good time: let him that moved you hither
Remove you hence. I knew you at the first,
198 You were a movable.
PETRUCHIO   Why, what's a movable?

---

180 *deny* refuse 181 *ask the banns* announce in church the intent to marry
184 *hard* (playing on *heard*, pronounced similarly) 187 *bonny* strapping
190 *dainties* delicacies; *cates* choice foods (playing, of course, on "Kates")
193 *sounded* proclaimed (with a play, in *deeply*, on "plumbed") 196 *In good
time* indeed 198 *movable* piece of furniture

KATE   A joint stool.   200
PETRUCHIO   Thou hast hit it: come sit on me.
KATE
Asses are made to bear, and so are you.
PETRUCHIO
Women are made to bear, and so are you.   203
KATE
No such jade as you, if me you mean.   204
PETRUCHIO
Alas, good Kate, I will not burden thee,
For knowing thee to be but young and light.   206
KATE
Too light for such a swain as you to catch,   207
And yet as heavy as my weight should be.   208
PETRUCHIO
Should be? should – buzz!   209
KATE   Well ta'en, and like a buzzard.
PETRUCHIO
O slow-winged turtle! Shall a buzzard take thee?   210
KATE
Ay, for a turtle, as he takes a buzzard.   211
PETRUCHIO
Come, come, you wasp, i' faith you are too angry.
KATE
If I be waspish best beware my sting.
PETRUCHIO
My remedy is then to pluck it out.

---

200 *joint stool* stool made by a joiner ("I took you for a joint stool" was a
standard joke, meaning "you're not worth noticing")   203 *bear* (1) bear children, (2) bear the weight of men in lovemaking   204 *jade* worthless horse
206 *For knowing* because I know; *light* (1) weak, (2) inconsequential, (3) flir-
tatious   207 *swain* peasant lover   208 *heavy . . . be* (the image is from
coinage: not counterfeit or cut down)   209 *buzz* (exclamation meaning
"nonsense," playing on *be[e]*); *buzzard* untrainable type of hawk, hence fool
210 *turtle* turtledove   211 *buzzard* (the term was applied to large moths and
beetles, insects that the dove doesn't like: the line means "you're a fool if you
think I'm a turtledove")

KATE
  Ay, if the fool could find it where it lies.

PETRUCHIO
  Who knows not where a wasp does wear his sting?
  In his tail.

KATE   In his tongue.

PETRUCHIO   Whose tongue?

KATE
220 Yours, if you talk of tales, and so farewell.

PETRUCHIO
  What, with my tongue in your tail?
  Nay, come again, good Kate, I am a gentleman.

KATE   That I'll try.
     She strikes him.

PETRUCHIO
  I swear I'll cuff you if you strike again.

KATE
225 So may you lose your arms.
  If you strike me you are no gentleman,
  And if no gentleman, why then no arms.

PETRUCHIO
228 A herald, Kate? O put me in thy books.

KATE
229 What is your crest, a coxcomb?

PETRUCHIO
230 A combless cock, so Kate will be my hen.

KATE
231 No cock of mine, you crow too like a craven.

PETRUCHIO
  Nay, come, Kate, come, you must not look so sour.

KATE
233 It is my fashion when I see a crab.

---

225 *arms* coat of arms 228 *in thy books* in your heraldic registers (playing
on "in your good graces") 229 *crest* armorial device; *coxcomb* cap of a court
fool (playing on *crest,* comb; Petruchio then quibbles on "cock's comb")
230 *combless* gentle (with "comb" or crest cut down) 231 *craven* cock that
will not fight 233 *crab* crab apple (notoriously sour)

PETRUCHIO
    Why, here's no crab, and therefore look not sour.
KATE
    There is, there is.
PETRUCHIO
    Then show it me.
KATE   Had I a glass I would.   236
PETRUCHIO   What, you mean my face?
KATE   Well aimed of such a young one.   238
PETRUCHIO
    Now, by Saint George, I am too young for you.
KATE
    Yet you are withered.   240
PETRUCHIO   'Tis with cares.
KATE   I care not.
PETRUCHIO
    Nay, hear you, Kate, in sooth you scape not so.   241
KATE
    I chafe you if I tarry; let me go.
PETRUCHIO
    No, not a whit. I find you passing gentle.
    'Twas told me you were rough and coy and sullen,   244
    And now I find report a very liar,
    For thou art pleasant, gamesome, passing courteous,
    But slow in speech, yet sweet as springtime flowers.
    Thou canst not frown, thou canst not look askance,   248
    Nor bite the lip as angry wenches will,
    Nor hast thou pleasure to be cross in talk.   250
    But thou with mildness entertain'st thy wooers,
    With gentle conference, soft and affable.
    Why does the world report that Kate doth limp?
    O sland'rous world! Kate like a hazel twig
    Is straight and slender, and as brown in hue
    As hazelnuts and sweeter than the kernels.

---

236 *glass* looking glass   238 *aimed of* guessed for; *young* inexperienced   241
sooth truth   244 *coy* haughty   248 *askance* scornfully

257   O let me see thee walk. Thou dost not halt.

KATE

258   Go, fool, and whom thou keep'st command.

PETRUCHIO

259   Did ever Dian so become a grove

260   As Kate this chamber with her princely gait?
      O be thou Dian and let her be Kate.

262   And then let Kate be chaste and Dian sportful.

KATE

      Where did you study all this goodly speech?

PETRUCHIO

264   It is extempore, from my mother wit.

KATE

265   A witty mother, witless else her son.

PETRUCHIO   Am I not wise?

267 KATE   Yes, keep you warm.

PETRUCHIO

      Marry, so I mean, sweet Katherine, in thy bed.
      And therefore, setting all this chat aside,

270   Thus in plain terms. Your father hath consented
      That you shall be my wife, your dowry 'greed upon,

272   And will you, nill you, I will marry you.

273   Now, Kate, I am a husband for your turn,
      For by this light, whereby I see thy beauty –
      Thy beauty that doth make me like thee well –
      Thou must be married to no man but me,

         Enter Baptista, Gremio, [and] Tranio [as Lucentio].

      For I am he am born to tame you, Kate,

278   And bring you from a wild Kate to a Kate
      Conformable as other household Kates.

---

257 *halt* limp   **258** *whom thou keep'st* i.e., your servants   **259** *Dian* Diana (goddess of virginity and of the hunt)   **262** *sportful* amorous   **264** *mother wit* native intelligence   **265** *witless . . . son* otherwise her son would be witless (his only wit being inherited from her)   **267** *keep you warm* i.e., take care of yourself (to have the wit or wisdom to keep warm being proverbial)   **272** *will you, nill you* whether you will or not   **273** *for your turn* to suit you   **278** *wild Kate* (punning on "wildcat")

Here comes your father. Never make denial,   280
I must and will have Katherine to my wife.

BAPTISTA

Now, Signor Petruchio, how speed you with my daugh-   282
ter?

PETRUCHIO

How but well, sir? How but well?
It were impossible I should speed amiss.

BAPTISTA

Why, how now, daughter Katherine? In your dumps?

KATE

Call you me daughter? Now, I promise you   286
You have showed a tender fatherly regard
To wish me wed to one half lunatic,
A madcap ruffian and a swearing Jack,
That thinks with oaths to face the matter out.   290

PETRUCHIO

Father, 'tis thus. Yourself and all the world
That talked of her have talked amiss of her.
If she be curst it is for policy,   293
For she's not froward but modest as the dove.
She is not hot but temperate as the morn.   295
For patience she will prove a second Grissel,   296
And Roman Lucrece for her chastity.   297
And, to conclude, we have 'greed so well together
That upon Sunday is the wedding day.

KATE

I'll see thee hanged on Sunday first.   300

GREMIO

Hark, Petruchio, she says she'll see thee hanged first.

---

282 *speed* succeed   286 *promise* assure   290 *face* brazen   293 *policy* cunning   295 *hot* of angry disposition   296 *Grissel* Griselda (the epitome of wifely patience and obedience; cf. Boccaccio's *Decameron*, X, 10, or Chaucer's Clerk's Tale)   297 *Lucrece* (she killed herself after being raped by Sextus Tarquinius, hence became the epitome of wifely chastity and honor; cf. Shakespeare's *The Rape of Lucrece*)

TRANIO

302   Is this your speeding? Nay, then good night our part!

PETRUCHIO

Be patient, gentlemen, I choose her for myself.
If she and I be pleased, what's that to you?
'Tis bargained 'twixt us twain, being alone,
That she shall still be curst in company.
I tell you, 'tis incredible to believe
How much she loves me. O the kindest Kate!
She hung about my neck, and kiss on kiss

310   She vied so fast, protesting oath on oath,
That in a twink she won me to her love.

312   O you are novices. 'Tis a world to see
How tame, when men and women are alone,

314   A meacock wretch can make the curstest shrew.
Give me thy hand, Kate, I will unto Venice

316   To buy apparel 'gainst the wedding day.
Provide the feast, father, and bid the guests.

318   I will be sure my Katherine shall be fine.

BAPTISTA

I know not what to say – but give me your hands.

320   God send you joy! Petruchio, 'tis a match.

GREMIO, TRANIO

Amen, say we, we will be witnesses.

PETRUCHIO

Father, and wife, and gentlemen, adieu.
I will to Venice. Sunday comes apace.
We will have rings and things and fine array,

325   And kiss me, Kate, *[Sings.]* "We will be married a Sunday."

Exeunt Petruchio and Kate [severally].

---

302 *speeding* success; *good . . . part* good-bye to our hopes (of marrying Bianca)   310 *vied* raised the bid (cardplaying term)   312 *world* i.e., worth a world   314 *meacock* cowardly   316 *'gainst* in anticipation of   318 *fine* finely dressed   325 s.d. *severally* at different doors

GREMIO

Was ever match clapped up so suddenly?   326

BAPTISTA

Faith, gentlemen, now I play a merchant's part

And venture madly on a desperate mart.   328

TRANIO

'Twas a commodity lay fretting by you.   329

'Twill bring you gain or perish on the seas.   330

BAPTISTA

The gain I seek is quiet in the match.

GREMIO

No doubt but he hath got a quiet catch.

But now, Baptista, to your younger daughter.

Now is the day we long have lookèd for.

I am your neighbor and was suitor first.

TRANIO

And I am one that love Bianca more

Than words can witness or your thoughts can guess.

GREMIO

Youngling, thou canst not love so dear as I.

TRANIO

Graybeard, thy love doth freeze.

GREMIO   But thine doth fry.

Skipper, stand back, 'tis age that nourisheth.   340

TRANIO

But youth in ladies' eyes that flourisheth.

BAPTISTA

Content you, gentlemen, I will compound this strife.   342

'Tis deeds must win the prize, and he of both   343

That can assure my daughter greatest dower   344

---

326 *match* contract (with a play on "mating"); *clapped up* shaken hands on, agreed to   328 *mart* bargain   329 *fretting* (of a stored commodity that decays, as wool "fretted" by moths; with a play on "chafing")   340 *Skipper* flighty youth   342 *compound* settle   343 *he of both* whichever of the two (of you)   344 *assure* guarantee; *dower* portion of the husband's estate left to the widow

Shall have Bianca's love.
Say, Signor Gremio, what can you assure her?

GREMIO
First, as you know, my house within the city
Is richly furnishèd with plate and gold,
349   Basins and ewers to lave her dainty hands;
350   My hangings all of Tyrian tapestry;
351   In ivory coffers I have stuffed my crowns;
352   In cypress chests my arras counterpoints,
353   Costly apparel, tents, and canopies,
354   Fine linen, Turkey cushions bossed with pearl,
355   Valance of Venice gold in needlework,
Pewter and brass, and all things that belongs
To house or housekeeping. Then at my farm
358   I have a hundred milk kine to the pail,
Six score fat oxen standing in my stalls,
360   And all things answerable to this portion.
361   Myself am struck in years, I must confess,
And if I die tomorrow this is hers,
If whilst I live she will be only mine.

TRANIO
That "only" came well in. Sir, list to me.
I am my father's heir and only son.
If I may have your daughter to my wife
I'll leave her houses three or four as good,
Within rich Pisa walls, as any one
Old Signor Gremio has in Padua,
370   Besides two thousand ducats by the year
371   Of fruitful land, all which shall be her jointure.
What, have I pinched you, Signor Gremio?

---

349 *lave* wash   350 *Tyrian* purple   351 *crowns* money   352 *arras counterpoints* quilted tapestry counterpanes   353 *tents, canopies* (types of bed hangings)   354 *bossed* embroidered   355 *Valance* drapery for the bed canopy   358 *milk kine . . . pail* dairy cows   360 *all . . . portion* all my possessions are equally valuable   361 *struck* advanced   370 *ducats* gold coins   371 *Of* i.e., the income from; *jointure* settlement

GREMIO

  Two thousand ducats by the year of land!

    [Aside]

  My land amounts not to so much in all.–

  That she shall have, besides an argosy   375

  That now is lying in Marseilles' road.   376

  What, have I choked you with an argosy?

TRANIO

  Gremio, 'tis known my father hath no less

  Than three great argosies, besides two galliasses   379

  And twelve tight galleys. These I will assure her   380

  And twice as much whate'er thou off'rest next.

GREMIO

  Nay, I have offered all, I have no more,

  And she can have no more than all I have.

  If you like me, she shall have me and mine.

TRANIO

  Why, then the maid is mine from all the world

  By your firm promise. Gremio is outvied.   386

BAPTISTA

  I must confess your offer is the best,

  And let your father make her the assurance,   388

  She is your own, else you must pardon me.

  If you should die before him, where's her dower?   *390*

TRANIO

  That's but a cavil. He is old, I young.

GREMIO

  And may not young men die as well as old?

BAPTISTA

  Well, gentlemen, I am thus resolved.

  On Sunday next, you know,

  My daughter Katherine is to be married.

  Now on the Sunday following shall Bianca

---

375 *argosy* large merchant ship   376 *Marseilles'* (pronounced "Marsellus");
road harbor   379 *galliasses* large galleys   380 *tight* sound, well caulked
386 *outvied* outbid   388 *assurance* guarantee

Be bride to you, if you make this assurance.
If not, to Signor Gremio.
And so I take my leave and thank you both.   *Exit.*
GREMIO
400   Adieu, good neighbor. Now I fear thee not.
401   Sirrah young gamester, your father were a fool
To give thee all and in his waning age
403   Set foot under thy table. Tut, a toy!
An old Italian fox is not so kind, my boy.   *Exit.*
TRANIO
A vengeance on your crafty withered hide!
406   Yet I have faced it with a card of ten.
'Tis in my head to do my master good.
I see no reason but supposed Lucentio
Must get a father, called supposed Vincentio;
410   And that's a wonder. Fathers commonly
411   Do get their children, but in this case of wooing
A child shall get a sire if I fail not of my cunning. *Exit.*

*

∾ **III.1** *Enter Lucentio [as Cambio], Hortensio
[as Litio], and Bianca.*

LUCENTIO
Fiddler, forbear, you grow too forward, sir.
Have you so soon forgot the entertainment
Her sister Katherine welcomed you withal?
HORTENSIO
But, wrangling pedant, this is
5   The patroness of heavenly harmony.
6   Then give me leave to have prerogative,
And when in music we have spent an hour

---

401 *Sirrah* (contemptuous to a person of equal rank); *were* would be **403**
Set . . . table i.e., become your dependent; *a toy* nonsense **406** *faced . . . ten*
bluffed successfully with a ten-spot **411** *get* beget
  III.1 Baptista's house **5** *patroness* goddess **6** *prerogative* precedence

Your lecture shall have leisure for as much.   8

LUCENTIO
Preposterous ass, that never read so far
To know the cause why music was ordained!   10
Was it not to refresh the mind of man
After his studies or his usual pain?
Then give me leave to read philosophy,   12
And while I pause, serve in your harmony.   13

HORTENSIO
Sirrah, I will not bear these braves of thine.   15

BIANCA
Why, gentlemen, you do me double wrong
To strive for that which resteth in my choice.
I am no breeching scholar in the schools.
I'll not be tied to hours nor 'pointed times,   18
But learn my lessons as I please myself.
And, to cut off all strife, here sit we down.   20
Take you your instrument, play you the whiles;
His lecture will be done ere you have tuned.   22

HORTENSIO
You'll leave his lecture when I am in tune?

LUCENTIO
That will be never. Tune your instrument.

BIANCA   Where left we last?

LUCENTIO   Here, madam:
   [Reads.]
            "Hic ibat Simois, hic est Sigeia tellus,
            Hic steterat Priami regia celsa senis."   28

BIANCA   Conster them.   30

---

8 *lecture* lesson   12 *pain* toil   13 *read* teach   15 *braves* insults   18 *breeching scholar* schoolboy liable to whipping   22 *the whiles* meanwhile   28–29 *Hic . . . senis* here flowed the Simois, here lies the Sigeian plain, here stood the lofty palace of old Priam (Ovid, *Epistolae Heroidum*, I, a letter from Penelope to Ulysses)   30 *Conster* construe (translate)

LUCENTIO   "Hic ibat," as I told you before; "Simois," I
am Lucentio; "hic est," son unto Vincentio of Pisa;
"Sigeia tellus," disguised thus to get your love; "Hic
steterat," and that Lucentio that comes a-wooing; "Pri-
35 ami," is my man Tranio; "regia," bearing my port;
36 "celsa senis," that we might beguile the old pantaloon.

HORTENSIO   Madam, my instrument's in tune.

38 BIANCA   Let's hear. *[He plays.]* O fie, the treble jars.

39 LUCENTIO   Spit in the hole, man, and tune again.

40 BIANCA   Now let me see if I can conster it.
"Hic ibat Simois," I know you not; "hic est Sigeia tellus," I trust you not; "Hic steterat Priami," take heed he
hear us not; "regia," presume not; "celsa senis," despair
not.

HORTENSIO
Madam, 'tis now in tune.

LUCENTIO   All but the bass.

HORTENSIO
The bass is right, 'tis the base knave that jars.
[Aside]
47 How fiery and forward our pedant is!
Now, for my life, the knave doth court my love.
49 Pedascule, I'll watch you better yet.

BIANCA
50 In time I may believe, yet I mistrust.

LUCENTIO
51 Mistrust it not, for sure Aeacides
52 Was Ajax, called so from his grandfather.

BIANCA
I must believe my master, else I promise you,
I should be arguing still upon that doubt.

---

35 *bearing my port* behaving as I would   36 *pantaloon* foolish old man   38
jars is discordant   39 *Spit in the hole* (to make the peg hold)   47 *pedant*
schoolmaster or tutor   49 *Pedascule* (Latin coinage from *pedant*, contemptu-
ously diminutive; four syllables)   51 *Aeacides* descendant of Aeacus (Lucentio explains a reference in the line of Ovid's epistle that follows immediately
after the two lines already quoted)   52 *Ajax* one of the Greek heroes at Troy

But let it rest. Now, Litio, to you.
Good master, take it not unkindly, pray,
That I have been thus pleasant with you both.

HORTENSIO
You may go walk and give me leave a while.
My lessons make no music in three parts.   59

LUCENTIO
Are you so formal, sir? *[Aside]* Well, I must wait   60
And watch withal, for but I be deceived,   61
Our fine musician groweth amorous.

HORTENSIO
Madam, before you touch the instrument
To learn the order of my fingering,
I must begin with rudiments of art,
To teach you gamut in a briefer sort,
More pleasant, pithy, and effectual   66
Than hath been taught by any of my trade.
And there it is in writing, fairly drawn.

BIANCA
Why, I am past my gamut long ago.   70

HORTENSIO
Yet read the gamut of Hortensio.

BIANCA   *[Reads.]*
        "*Gamut* I am, the ground of all accord,   72
        A re, to plead Hortensio's passion;
        B mi, Bianca, take him for thy lord,
        C fa ut, that loves with all affection;   75
        D sol re, one clef, two notes have I;
        E la mi, show pity or I die."
Call you this gamut? Tut, I like it not.

---

59 *in three parts* for three voices 60 *formal* precise 61 *withal* at the same time; *but* unless 66 *gamut* the scale 71 s.d. *Reads* (she intones each line on the appropriate note) 72 *ground* (*gamut* is also the lowest note, or ground, of the scale; also called *ut,* as in l. 75, or, in modern terminology, "do"); *accord* harmony 75–77 *ut, re, mi* (repeated because a second scale starts at C)

79 Old fashions please me best; I am not so nice
80 To change true rules for odd inventions.
     Enter a Messenger.

MESSENGER
  Mistress, your father prays you leave your books
  And help to dress your sister's chamber up.
  You know tomorrow is the wedding day.

BIANCA
  Farewell, sweet masters both, I must be gone.
                    [Exeunt Bianca and Messenger.]

LUCENTIO
  Faith, mistress, then I have no cause to stay.   *[Exit.]*

HORTENSIO
  But I have cause to pry into this pedant.
  Methinks he looks as though he were in love.
  Yet if thy thoughts, Bianca, be so humble
89 To cast thy wand'ring eyes on every stale,
90 Seize thee that list. If once I find thee ranging,
91 Hortensio will be quit with thee by changing.   *Exit.*

*

✺ **III.2** *Enter Baptista, Gremio, Tranio [as Lucentio],
    Kate, Bianca, [Lucentio as Cambio,] and others
    (Attendants).*

BAPTISTA   *[To Tranio]*
  Signor Lucentio, this is the 'pointed day
  That Katherine and Petruchio should be married,
  And yet we hear not of our son-in-law.
  What will be said? What mockery will it be
5 To want the bridegroom when the priest attends
  To speak the ceremonial rites of marriage?

---

79 *nice* capricious   89 *stale* decoy, bait   90 *Seize . . . list* let him take you
that pleases; *ranging* straying   91 *be quit* get even; *changing* i.e., to another
love
  III.2 Before Baptista's house   5 *want* lack

What says Lucentio to this shame of ours?

KATE

No shame but mine. I must, forsooth, be forced 8
To give my hand opposed against my heart
Unto a mad-brain rudesby, full of spleen, 10
Who wooed in haste and means to wed at leisure.
I told you, I, he was a frantic fool,
Hiding his bitter jests in blunt behavior.
And to be noted for a merry man, 14
He'll woo a thousand, 'point the day of marriage,
Make friends, invite, and proclaim the banns,
Yet never means to wed where he hath wooed.
Now must the world point at poor Katherine
And say, "Lo, there is mad Petruchio's wife,
If it would please him come and marry her." 20

TRANIO

Patience, good Katherine, and Baptista too.
Upon my life, Petruchio means but well,
Whatever fortune stays him from his word.
Though he be blunt, I know him passing wise;
Though he be merry, yet withal he's honest. 25

KATE

Would Katherine had never seen him though!

Exit weeping.

BAPTISTA

Go, girl, I cannot blame thee now to weep,
For such an injury would vex a very saint,
Much more a shrew of thy impatient humor. 29
Enter Biondello.

BIONDELLO Master, master, old news! And such news as 30
you never heard of!

BAPTISTA Is it new and old too? How may that be?

---

8 *forsooth* indeed **10** *rudesby* boor; *spleen* capriciousness **14** *noted for* known as **25** *withal* at the same time **29** *humor* disposition **30** *old* great, rare (Baptista misunderstands)

BIONDELLO   Why, is it not news to hear of Petruchio's
coming?

BAPTISTA   Is he come?

BIONDELLO   Why, no, sir.

BAPTISTA   What then?

BIONDELLO   He is coming.

BAPTISTA   When will he be here?

40   BIONDELLO   When he stands where I am and sees you
there.

42   TRANIO   But say, what to thine old news?

BIONDELLO   Why, Petruchio is coming, in a new hat and
44   an old jerkin; a pair of old breeches thrice turned; a pair
45   of boots that have been candle cases, one buckled, another laced; an old rusty sword ta'en out of the town ar-
47   mory, with a broken hilt and chapeless; with two
48   broken points; his horse hipped – with an old mothy
49   saddle and stirrups of no kindred – besides, possessed
50   with the glanders and like to mose in the chine; trou-
51   bled with the lampas, infected with the fashions, full of
52   windgalls, sped with spavins, rayed with the yellows,
53   past cure of the fives, stark spoiled with the staggers,
54   begnawn with the bots, swayed in the back, and
55   shoulder-shotten; near-legged before, and with a half-
56   checked bit and a headstall of sheep's leather which,

----

42 *to* about   44 *jerkin* jacket   45 *candle cases* (worn-out boots were sometimes hung on the wall to hold candle ends and the like)   47 *chapeless* without the metal plate on the scabbard covering the sword point   48 *points*
laces holding up his breeches; *hipped* lamed in the hip   49 *possessed* afflicted
50 *glanders* horse disease affecting the nose and mouth; *mose . . . chine* grow
weak in the back (chine is the spine, but mose has not been satisfactorily explained)   51 *lampas* infected mouth; *fashions* (or "farcins") equine ulcera-
tions   52 *windgalls* leg tumors; *sped . . . spavins* destroyed by inflammations
of the joints; *rayed . . . yellows* streaked with jaundice   53 *fives* (or "avives")
swelling of the glands behind the ears; *stark* utterly; *staggers* equine palsy   54
begnawn . . . bots eaten up by intestinal worms   55 *shoulder-shotten* weak in
the shoulder; *near-legged before* knock-kneed in front   55–56 *half-checked
bit* bit that is only halfway effective   56 *headstall* part of the bridle going
around the head; *sheep's leather* (inferior to pigskin)

being restrained to keep him from stumbling, hath   57
been often burst and new-repaired with knots; one
girth six times pieced, and a woman's crupper of velure   59
which hath two letters for her name fairly set down in   60
studs, and here and there pieced with packthread.   61

BAPTISTA   Who comes with him?

BIONDELLO   O sir, his lackey, for all the world caparisoned like the horse: with a linen stock on one leg   64
and a kersey boothose on the other, gartered with a red   65
and blue list; an old hat and the humor of forty fancies   66
pricked in't for a feather – a monster, a very monster in   67
apparel, and not like a Christian footboy or a gentle-   68
man's lackey.

TRANIO
'Tis some odd humor pricks him to this fashion,   70
Yet oftentimes he goes but mean-appareled.

BAPTISTA   I am glad he's come, howsoe'er he comes.

BIONDELLO   Why, sir, he comes not.

BAPTISTA   Didst thou not say he comes?

BIONDELLO   Who? That Petruchio came?

BAPTISTA   Ay, that Petruchio came.

BIONDELLO   No, sir, I say his horse comes, with him on
his back.

BAPTISTA   Why, that's all one.

BIONDELLO   *[Sings.]*   79

Nay, by Saint Jamy,   *80*
I hold you a penny,   81

---

57 *restrained* drawn back   59 *pieced* patched; *crupper* strap that passes under
the horse's tail to keep the saddle in place; *velure* velvet (the crupper would
normally be of leather; a velvet one would be largely useless for serious riding)   60 *two letters* (the initials of the woman whose velvet crupper Petruchio is using)   61 *pieced* tied together   64 *stock* stocking   65 *kersey boothose*
coarse woolen overstocking   66 *list* strip of cloth; *humor . . . fancies* (not satisfactorily explained: presumably a wildly fanciful decoration)   67 *pricked*
pinned   68 *footboy* page   70 *humor* whim; *pricks* drives   79 *all one* the
same thing   81 *hold* bet

A horse and a man
Is more than one
And yet not many.

Enter Petruchio and Grumio.

PETRUCHIO
  Come, where be these gallants? Who's at home?

BAPTISTA
  You are welcome, sir.

PETRUCHIO   And yet I come not well.

87 BAPTISTA   And yet you halt not.

TRANIO   Not so well appareled as I wish you were.

PETRUCHIO
89 Were it better, I should rush in thus.
90 But where is Kate? Where is my lovely bride?
  How does my father? Gentles, methinks you frown.
  And wherefore gaze this goodly company
  As if they saw some wondrous monument,
94 Some comet or unusual prodigy?

BAPTISTA
  Why, sir, you know this is your wedding day.
  First were we sad, fearing you would not come,
97 Now sadder that you come so unprovided.
98 Fie, doff this habit, shame to your estate,
  An eyesore to our solemn festival.

TRANIO
100 And tell us what occasion of import
  Hath all so long detained you from your wife
  And sent you hither so unlike yourself?

PETRUCHIO
  Tedious it were to tell and harsh to hear.
  Sufficeth I am come to keep my word,
105 Though in some part enforcèd to digress,

---

87 *halt* limp (Baptista quibbles on *come* in the sense of "walk") 89 *it* i.e.,
my apparel 94 *prodigy* unnatural phenomenon 97 *unprovided* improperly
equipped 98 *habit* clothing; *estate* social position 105 *digress* deviate
(from his intention to dress well; see II.1.316)

Which at more leisure I will so excuse
As you shall well be satisfied with all.
But where is Kate? I stay too long from her.
The morning wears, 'tis time we were at church.   109

TRANIO

See not your bride in these unreverent robes.   110
Go to my chamber; put on clothes of mine.

PETRUCHIO

Not I, believe me. Thus I'll visit her.

BAPTISTA

But thus, I trust, you will not marry her?

PETRUCHIO

Good sooth, even thus. Therefore ha' done with words.   114
To me she's married, not unto my clothes.
Could I repair what she will wear in me   116
As I can change these poor accoutrements,
'Twere well for Kate and better for myself.
But what a fool am I to chat with you
When I should bid good morrow to my bride   120
And seal the title with a lovely kiss.   121

                              Exit [with Grumio].

TRANIO

He hath some meaning in his mad attire.
We will persuade him, be it possible,
To put on better ere he go to church.

BAPTISTA

I'll after him and see the event of this.   125

              Exit [with Bianca, Gremio, and Attendants].

TRANIO

But sir, to love concerneth us to add   126
Her father's liking, which to bring to pass,
As I before imparted to your worship,

---

109 *wears* is passing 114 *Good sooth* indeed 116 *wear* wear out 121 *seal
the title* confirm my rights; *lovely* loving 125 *event* outcome 126–27 *to
love . . . liking* i.e., to woo Bianca successfully we need her father's approval
in addition (the speech appears to begin in the middle of the conversation)

I am to get a man – whate'er he be
130   It skills not much, we'll fit him to our turn –
And he shall be Vincentio of Pisa,
132   And make assurance here in Padua
Of greater sums than I have promisèd.
So shall you quietly enjoy your hope
And marry sweet Bianca with consent.

LUCENTIO
Were it not that my fellow schoolmaster
137   Doth watch Bianca's steps so narrowly,
138   'Twere good, methinks, to steal our marriage,
Which once performed, let all the world say no,
140   I'll keep mine own despite of all the world.

TRANIO
That by degrees we mean to look into
142   And watch our vantage in this business.
We'll overreach the graybeard, Gremio,
The narrow-prying father, Minola,
145   The quaint musician, amorous Litio –
All for my master's sake, Lucentio.
    Enter Gremio.
Signor Gremio, come you from the church?

GREMIO
As willingly as e'er I came from school.

TRANIO
And is the bride and bridegroom coming home?

GREMIO
150   A bridegroom, say you? 'Tis a groom indeed,
A grumbling groom, and that the girl shall find.

TRANIO
Curster than she? Why, 'tis impossible.

---

130 *skills* matters; *turn* purpose 132 *make assurance* give guarantees 137
narrowly closely 138 *steal . . . marriage* elope 142 *watch our vantage* look
out for our opportunity 145 *quaint* crafty 150 *groom* (quibbling on "servant," "boor")

GREMIO
  Why, he's a devil, a devil, a very fiend.
TRANIO
  Why, she's a devil, a devil, the devil's dam.   154
GREMIO
  Tut, she's a lamb, a dove, a fool to him.   155
  I'll tell you, Sir Lucentio. When the priest
  Did ask if Katherine should be his wife,
  "Ay, by gogs wouns," quoth he, and swore so loud   158
  That, all amazed, the priest let fall the book,
  And as he stooped again to take it up   *160*
  This mad-brained bridegroom took him such a cuff   161
  That down fell priest and book, and book and priest.
  "Now, take them up," quoth he, "if any list."   163
TRANIO
  What said the wench when he rose again?
GREMIO
  Trembled and shook, for why he stamped and swore,   165
  As if the vicar meant to cozen him.   166
  But after many ceremonies done
  He calls for wine. "A health!" quoth he, as if
  He had been aboard, carousing to his mates
  After a storm; quaffed off the muscadel   170
  And threw the sops all in the sexton's face,   171
  Having no other reason
  But that his beard grew thin and hungerly   173
  And seemed to ask him sops as he was drinking.   174
  This done, he took the bride about the neck
  And kissed her lips with such a clamorous smack
  That at the parting all the church did echo.

---

154 *dam* mother   155 *a fool to* an innocent compared with   158 *by gogs wouns* by God's (Christ's) wounds   161 *took* gave   163 *take* pick; *if any list* if anyone pleases   165 *for why* because   166 *cozen* cheat (with an invalid ceremony)   170 *muscadel* (or muscatel) a sweet wine (Petruchio should be offering it to the guests, not drinking it himself)   171 *sops* cakes dipped in the wine   173 *hungerly* sparsely   174 *ask him* ask him for

I, seeing this, came thence for very shame,
179 And after me, I know, the rout is coming.
180 Such a mad marriage never was before.
Hark, hark, I hear the minstrels play.
  Music plays.
  Enter Petruchio, Kate, Bianca, Hortensio [as Litio],
  Baptista [, and Grumio, with Attendants].

PETRUCHIO
Gentlemen and friends, I thank you for your pains.
I know you think to dine with me today
184 And have prepared great store of wedding cheer,
But so it is, my haste doth call me hence
And therefore here I mean to take my leave.

BAPTISTA
Is't possible you will away tonight?

PETRUCHIO
I must away today, before night come.
189 Make it no wonder. If you knew my business
190 You would entreat me rather go than stay.
And, honest company, I thank you all,
That have beheld me give away myself
To this most patient, sweet, and virtuous wife.
Dine with my father, drink a health to me,
For I must hence; and farewell to you all.

TRANIO
Let us entreat you stay till after dinner.

PETRUCHIO
It may not be.

GREMIO   Let me entreat you.

PETRUCHIO
It cannot be.

200 KATE   Let me entreat you.

PETRUCHIO
I am content.

KATE   Are you content to stay?

---

179 *rout* mob   184 *cheer* entertainment   189 *Make* consider

PETRUCHIO

    I am content you shall entreat me stay,

    But yet not stay, entreat me how you can.

KATE

    Now if you love me, stay.   204

PETRUCHIO   Grumio, my horse!

GRUMIO   Ay, sir, they be ready; the oats have eaten the   205
horses.

KATE

    Nay then,

    Do what thou canst, I will not go today,

    No, nor tomorrow nor till I please myself.

    The door is open, sir, there lies your way;   210

    You may be jogging whiles your boots are green.   211

    For me, I'll not be gone till I please myself.

    'Tis like you'll prove a jolly surly groom,   213

    That take it on you at the first so roundly.   214

PETRUCHIO

    O Kate, content thee; prithee, be not angry.

KATE

    I will be angry. What hast thou to do?   216

    Father, be quiet, he shall stay my leisure.

GREMIO

    Ay, marry, sir, now it begins to work.

KATE

    Gentlemen, forward to the bridal dinner.

    I see a woman may be made a fool   220

    If she had not a spirit to resist.

PETRUCHIO

    They shall go forward, Kate, at thy command.

    Obey the bride, you that attend on her,

    Go to the feast, revel and domineer,   224

---

204 *horse* horses (old plural)   205–6 *the oats . . . horses* (Grumio gets it back-
wards)   211 *You may . . . green* (proverbial for getting an early start); *green*
i.e., fresh   213 *jolly* arrogant   214 *take it on you* assert yourself; *roundly*
unceremoniously   216 *What . . . do* what business is it of yours   224 *domi-
neer* carouse

Carouse full measure to her maidenhead,
Be mad and merry or go hang yourselves.
But for my bonny Kate, she must with me.
228 Nay, look not big, nor stamp, nor stare, nor fret;
I will be master of what is mine own.
230 She is my goods, my chattels; she is my house,
My household stuff, my field, my barn,
My horse, my ox, my ass, my anything;
And here she stands, touch her whoever dare.
234 I'll bring mine action on the proudest he
That stops my way in Padua. Grumio,
Draw forth thy weapon, we are beset with thieves.
Rescue thy mistress, if thou be a man.
Fear not, sweet wench; they shall not touch thee, Kate.
239 I'll buckler thee against a million.
Exeunt Petruchio, Kate [, and Grumio].

BAPTISTA
240 Nay, let them go, a couple of quiet ones.

GREMIO
Went they not quickly, I should die with laughing.

TRANIO
Of all mad matches never was the like.

LUCENTIO
Mistress, what's your opinion of your sister?

BIANCA
That being mad herself, she's madly mated.

GREMIO
I warrant him, Petruchio is Kated.

BAPTISTA
246 Neighbors and friends, though bride and bridegroom
wants
For to supply the places at the table,

---

228 *big* threatening **230–32** *my house . . . ass* (echoing the Tenth Commandment, "Thou shalt not covet thy neighbor's house, . . . nor his ox, nor his ass . . .") **234** *action* lawsuit **239** *buckler* shield **246** *wants* are missing

You know there wants no junkets at the feast.   248
Lucentio, you supply the bridegroom's place,
And let Bianca take her sister's room.   250

TRANIO

Shall sweet Bianca practice how to bride it?

BAPTISTA

She shall, Lucentio. Come, gentlemen, let's go. *Exeunt.*

*

∾ **IV.1** *Enter Grumio.*

GRUMIO Fie, fie, on all tired jades, on all mad masters,   1
and all foul ways! Was ever man so beaten? Was ever   2
man so rayed? Was ever man so weary? I am sent before   3
to make a fire, and they are coming after to warm
them. Now were not I a little pot and soon hot, my   5
very lips might freeze to my teeth, my tongue to the
roof of my mouth, my heart in my belly, ere I should
come by a fire to thaw me. But I with blowing the fire
shall warm myself, for considering the weather, a taller   9
man than I will take cold. Holla, ho! Curtis.   10
  Enter Curtis (a Servant).

CURTIS Who is that calls so coldly?

GRUMIO A piece of ice. If thou doubt it, thou mayst   11
slide from my shoulder to my heel with no greater a
run but my head and my neck. A fire, good Curtis.

CURTIS Is my master and his wife coming, Grumio?

GRUMIO O ay, Curtis, ay, and therefore fire, fire; cast on   16
no water.

CURTIS Is she so hot a shrew as she's reported?

GRUMIO She was, good Curtis, before this frost. But
thou know'st winter tames man, woman, and beast, for   20

---

248 *junkets* delicacies 250 *room* place
  IV.1 Petruchio's country house 1 *jades* worthless horses 2 *ways* roads
3 *rayed* dirtied 5 *a little . . . hot* (proverbial for a small person easily an-
gered) 9 *taller* better 11 *is that* is it who 16–17 *fire . . . water* (alluding
to the popular round "Scotland's Burning": "Fire, fire! Cast on water!")

it hath tamed my old master and my new mistress and myself, fellow Curtis.

23 CURTIS   Away, you three-inch fool! I am no beast.

24 GRUMIO   Am I but three inches? Why, thy horn is a foot, and so long am I at the least. But wilt thou make a fire or shall I complain on thee to our mistress, whose hand – she being now at hand – thou shalt soon feel, to 28 thy cold comfort, for being slow in thy hot office?

CURTIS   I prithee, good Grumio, tell me, how goes the 30 world?

GRUMIO   A cold world, Curtis, in every office but thine, 32 and therefore fire. Do thy duty, and have thy duty, for my master and mistress are almost frozen to death.

CURTIS   There's fire ready, and therefore, good Grumio, the news.

GRUMIO   Why, *[Sings.]* "Jack boy, ho boy," and as much news as thou wilt.

38 CURTIS   Come, you are so full of cony-catching.

GRUMIO   Why therefore fire, for I have caught extreme 40 cold. Where's the cook? Is supper ready, the house 41 trimmed, rushes strewed, cobwebs swept, the serving-42 men in their new fustian and white stockings, and 43 every officer his wedding garment on? Be the jacks fair 44 within, the jills fair without, the carpets laid, and every-thing in order?

CURTIS   All ready, and therefore, I pray thee, news.

GRUMIO   First, know my horse is tired, my master and mistress fall'n out.

CURTIS   How?

---

23 *three-inch* i.e., very short; *I am no beast* (Grumio having called himself a beast and Curtis his *fellow*)   24 *horn* i.e., of a cuckold   28 *hot office* task of providing heat   32 *have thy duty* have thy due, reward (proverbial)   38 *cony-catching* trickery (a cony being a rabbit; with a play on *Jack boy, ho boy,* a "catch" or round)   41 *rushes strewed* i.e., on the floor (the normal floor covering)   42 *fustian* coarse cotton cloth   43 *jacks* leather drinking vessels (playing on "fellows," servingmen)   44 *jills* metal measuring cups (playing on "girls," maidservants); *carpets* table covers

GRUMIO   Out of their saddles into the dirt – and thereby   *50*
hangs a tale.

CURTIS   Let's ha't, good Grumio.

GRUMIO   Lend thine ear.

CURTIS   Here.

GRUMIO   There.
    [Strikes him.]

CURTIS   This is to feel a tale, not to hear a tale.

GRUMIO   And therefore 'tis called a sensible tale, and this   *57*
cuff was but to knock at your ear and beseech listening.
Now I begin. Imprimis, we came down a foul hill, my   *59*
master riding behind my mistress –   *60*

CURTIS   Both of one horse?   *61*

GRUMIO   What's that to thee?

CURTIS   Why, a horse.

GRUMIO   Tell thou the tale – but hadst thou not crossed   *64*
me thou shouldst have heard how her horse fell, and
she under her horse; thou shouldst have heard in how
miry a place; how she was bemoiled, how he left her   *67*
with the horse upon her, how he beat me because her
horse stumbled, how she waded through the dirt to
pluck him off me; how he swore, how she prayed, that   *70*
never prayed before; how I cried, how the horses ran
away, how her bridle was burst; how I lost my
crupper – with many things of worthy memory, which
now shall die in oblivion, and thou return unexperi-   *74*
enced to thy grave.

CURTIS   By this reck'ning he is more shrew than she.

GRUMIO   Ay, and that thou and the proudest of you all
shall find when he comes home. But what talk I of this?   *78*
Call forth Nathaniel, Joseph, Nicholas, Philip, Walter,
Sugarsop, and the rest. Let their heads be sleekly   *80*

---

57 *sensible* (playing on "capable of being felt")   59 *Imprimis* first   61 *of* on
64 *crossed* interrupted   67 *bemoiled* bemired   74–75 *unexperienced* (hence
ignorant)   78 *what* why

81 combed, their blue coats brushed, and their garters of
82 an indifferent knit. Let them curtsy with their left legs
    and not presume to touch a hair of my master's horse-
    tail till they kiss their hands. Are they all ready?

CURTIS They are.

GRUMIO Call them forth.

CURTIS Do you hear, ho! You must meet my master to
88 countenance my mistress.

GRUMIO Why, she hath a face of her own.

90 CURTIS Who knows not that?

GRUMIO Thou, it seems, that calls for company to coun-
    tenance her.

93 CURTIS I call them forth to credit her.

        Enter four or five Servingmen.

GRUMIO Why, she comes to borrow nothing of them.

NATHANIEL Welcome home, Grumio!

PHILIP How now, Grumio?

JOSEPH What, Grumio!

NICHOLAS Fellow Grumio!

NATHANIEL How now, old lad!

100 GRUMIO Welcome, you; how now, you; what, you; fel-
    low, you; and thus much for greeting. Now, my spruce
    companions, is all ready and all things neat?

NATHANIEL All things is ready. How near is our master?

104 GRUMIO E'en at hand, alighted by this. And therefore be
105 not – Cock's passion, silence, I hear my master.

        Enter Petruchio and Kate.

PETRUCHIO
    Where be these knaves? What, no man at door
    To hold my stirrup nor to take my horse?
    Where is Nathaniel, Gregory, Philip?

---

81 *blue coats* (dark blue was the usual color of a servant's dress) 82 *indifferent* (either not different, matching, or any knit whatever); *curtsy . . . legs* (like
kissing their hands, below, absurdly elaborate forms of welcome) 88 *countenance* do honor to (Grumio then quibbles on countenance as *face*) 93
credit pay respect to (Grumio then quibbles on the financial sense) 104 *this*
this time 105 *Cock's passion* God's (Christ's) passion (on the Cross)

ALL SERVINGMEN   Here, here, sir; here, sir.
PETRUCHIO
  Here, sir; here, sir; here, sir; here, sir!   *110*
  You loggerheaded and unpolished grooms!   *111*
  What, no attendance? No regard? No duty?
  Where is the foolish knave I sent before.
GRUMIO
  Here, sir, as foolish as I was before.
PETRUCHIO
  You peasant swain, you whoreson malt-horse drudge!   *115*
  Did I not bid thee meet me in the park   *116*
  And bring along these rascal knaves with thee?
GRUMIO
  Nathaniel's coat, sir, was not fully made,
  And Gabriel's pumps were all unpinked i' th' heel.   *119*
  There was no link to color Peter's hat,   *120*
  And Walter's dagger was not come from sheathing.
  There were none fine but Adam, Rafe, and Gregory;   *122*
  The rest were ragged, old, and beggarly.
  Yet, as they are, here are they come to meet you.
PETRUCHIO
  Go, rascals, go, and fetch my supper in.

                                          Exeunt Servants.

    [Sings.]
            "Where is the life that late I led?
            Where are those –?"   *127*
  Sit down, Kate,
    [They sit at table.]
  And welcome. Food, food, food, food!
    Enter Servants with supper.
  Why, when, I say? – Nay, good sweet Kate, be merry.   *130*

---

111 *loggerheaded* blockheaded 115 *swain* lout; *whoreson* contemptible;
malt-horse drudge brewer's horse (which ploddingly turns a grain mill) 116
park deer park 119 *unpinked* without their ornamental patterns 120 *link*
torch (the smoke was used to blacken hats) 122 *fine* well turned out 127
Where are those (the ballad continues, "Where are those pleasant days?")

Off with my boots, you rogues! You villains, when?
   [Sings.]
         "It was the friar of orders gray,
            As he forth walkèd on his way" –
Out, you rogue! You pluck my foot awry.
   [Strikes him.]

135 Take that, and mend the plucking off the other.
Be merry, Kate. Some water here, what ho!
   Enter one with water.
Where's my spaniel Troilus? Sirrah, get you hence
And bid my cousin Ferdinand come hither –
                    [Exit Servant.]
One, Kate, that you must kiss and be acquainted with.

140 Where are my slippers? Shall I have some water?
Come, Kate, and wash, and welcome heartily.
You whoreson villain, will you let it fall?
   [Strikes him.]

KATE
Patience, I pray you, 'twas a fault unwilling.

PETRUCHIO
144 A whoreson, beetle-headed, flap-eared knave!
145 Come, Kate, sit down; I know you have a stomach.
146 Will you give thanks, sweet Kate, or else shall I?
What's this, mutton?

148 FIRST SERVANT Ay.

PETRUCHIO Who brought it?

150 PETER I.

PETRUCHIO
'Tis burnt, and so is all the meat.
What dogs are these! Where is the rascal cook?

---

135 *mend* do better at **144** *beetle-headed* blockheaded, stupid (the "head" of a "beetle," or mallet, being a heavy block of wood) **145** *stomach* appetite (playing on "temper") **146** *give thanks* i.e., say grace **148** *FIRST SERVANT* (Curtis or Peter)

How durst you, villains, bring it from the dresser,   153
And serve it thus to me that love it not?
    [He throws it at them.]
There, take it to you, trenchers, cups, and all.   155
You heedless joltheads and unmannered slaves!
What, do you grumble? I'll be with you straight.   157
                        [Exeunt Servants.]

KATE
I pray you, husband, be not so disquiet.
The meat was well if you were so contented.

PETRUCHIO
I tell thee, Kate, 'twas burnt and dried away,   160
And I expressly am forbid to touch it,
For it engenders choler, planteth anger,   162
And better 'twere that both of us did fast,
Since of ourselves, ourselves are choleric,
Than feed it with such overroasted flesh.   165
Be patient. Tomorrow't shall be mended,
And for this night we'll fast in company.
Come, I will bring thee to thy bridal chamber. *Exeunt.* 168
    Enter Servants severally.

NATHANIEL   Peter, didst ever see the like?
PETER   He kills her in her own humor.   170
    Enter Curtis.
GRUMIO   Where is he?
CURTIS   In her chamber, making a sermon of continency
to her,
And rails and swears and rates, that she, poor soul,   174
Knows not which way to stand, to look, to speak,
And sits as one new-risen from a dream.

---

153 *dresser* sideboard 155 *trenchers* wooden plates 157 *with you* even with
you 162 *choler* that "humor" (hot and dry) which produces anger (roast
meat was to be avoided by persons of such disposition) 165 *it* i.e., their
choler 168 s.d. *severally* at different doors 170 *kills . . . humor* subdues her
by acting like her 174 *rates* berates; *that* so that

Away, away, for he is coming hither.   *[Exeunt.]*
   Enter Petruchio.

PETRUCHIO
178   Thus have I politicly begun my reign,
   And 'tis my hope to end successfully.
180   My falcon now is sharp and passing empty,
181   And till she stoop she must not be full-gorged,
182   For then she never looks upon her lure.
183   Another way I have to man my haggard,
   To make her come and know her keeper's call:
185   That is, to watch her as we watch these kites
186   That bate and beat and will not be obedient.
   She ate no meat today, nor none shall eat.
   Last night she slept not, nor tonight she shall not.
   As with the meat, some undeservèd fault
190   I'll find about the making of the bed,
191   And here I'll fling the pillow, there the bolster,
   This way the coverlet, another way the sheets.
193   Ay, and amid this hurly I intend
   That all is done in reverent care of her.
   And in conclusion she shall watch all night,
   And if she chance to nod I'll rail and brawl
   And with the clamor keep her still awake.
198   This is a way to kill a wife with kindness,
199   And thus I'll curb her mad and headstrong humor.
200   He that knows better how to tame a shrew,
   Now let him speak: 'tis charity to show.   *Exit.*

*

---

178 *politicly* cunningly 180 *sharp* starved 181 *stoop* fly to and seize the lure (playing on "bow to authority") 182 *lure* decoy bird used to recall a hawk 183 *man* tame (hawking term, with a quibble); *haggard* wild female hawk 185 *watch* keep awake (as in taming a wild hawk); *kites* inferior hawks 186 *bate and beat* flutter and flap the wings 191 *bolster* long narrow cushion supporting the pillow 193 *intend* pretend 198 *kill . . . kindness* (ironically, referring to the proverb for spoiling a wife through overindulgence) 199 *humor* disposition 200 *shrew* (pronounced "shrow"; a rhyme with *show*)

❧ **IV.2** *Enter Tranio [as Lucentio] and Hortensio [as Litio].*

TRANIO
    Is't possible, friend Litio, that Mistress Bianca
    Doth fancy any other but Lucentio?
    I tell you, sir, she bears me fair in hand.   3
HORTENSIO
    Sir, to satisfy you in what I have said,
    Stand by and mark the manner of his teaching.
      [They stand aside.]
      Enter Bianca [and Lucentio as Cambio].
LUCENTIO
    Now mistress, profit you in what you read?   6
BIANCA
    What, master, read you? First resolve me that.   7
LUCENTIO
    I read that I profess, *The Art to Love.*   8
BIANCA
    And may you prove, sir, master of your art.   9
LUCENTIO
    While you, sweet dear, prove mistress of my heart.   10
      [They stand aside.]
HORTENSIO   *[Advancing with Tranio]*
    Quick proceeders, marry! Now tell me, I pray,   11
    You that durst swear that your mistress Bianca
    Loved none in the world so well as Lucentio —
TRANIO
    O despiteful love, unconstant womankind!
    I tell thee, Litio, this is wonderful.   14
                                                                 15

IV.2 Before Baptista's house **3** *bears . . . hand* encourages me **6** *read* study
7 *read* (quibbling on "teach"); *resolve* answer **8** *that I profess* what I'm an ex-
pert on; *The Art to Love* Ovid's *Ars amatoria* **9** *master . . . art* (quibbling on
the "M.A. degree") **11** *proceeders* degree candidates; *marry* indeed (originally an oath on the name of the Virgin Mary) **14** *despiteful* spiteful **15**
wonderful amazing

HORTENSIO
    Mistake no more: I am not Litio,
    Nor a musician, as I seem to be,
    But one that scorn to live in this disguise,
    For such a one as leaves a gentleman
20 And makes a god of such a cullion.
    Know, sir, that I am called Hortensio.

TRANIO
    Signor Hortensio, I have often heard
    Of your entire affection to Bianca,
24 And since mine eyes are witness of her lightness
    I will, with you, if you be so contented,
    Forswear Bianca and her love forever.

HORTENSIO
    See how they kiss and court. Signor Lucentio,
    Here is my hand and here I firmly vow
    Never to woo her more, but do forswear her,
30 As one unworthy all the former favors
31 That I have fondly flattered her withal.

TRANIO
    And here I take the like unfeignèd oath,
    Never to marry with her though she would entreat.
34 Fie on her, see how beastly she doth court him.

HORTENSIO
35 Would all the world but he had quite forsworn.
    For me, that I may surely keep mine oath,
    I will be married to a wealthy widow
    Ere three days pass, which hath as long loved me
39 As I have loved this proud disdainful haggard.
40 And so farewell, Signor Lucentio.
    Kindness in women, not their beauteous looks,
    Shall win my love – and so I take my leave,
    In resolution as I swore before.   *[Exit.]*

_____
20 *cullion* scoundrel (the schoolmaster) 24 *lightness* inconstancy 31 *fondly*
foolishly 34 *beastly* lasciviously 35 *Would . . . forsworn* i.e., would that he
were my only competition 39 *haggard* wild hawk

TRANIO
     Mistress Bianca, bless you with such grace
     As 'longeth to a lover's blessed case.
     Nay, I have ta'en you napping, gentle love,
     And have forsworn you with Hortensio.
BIANCA   *[Advancing]*
     Tranio, you jest. But have you both forsworn me?   48
TRANIO
     Mistress, we have.
LUCENTIO   Then we are rid of Litio.
TRANIO
     I' faith, he'll have a lusty widow now,   50
     That shall be wooed and wedded in a day.
BIANCA
     God give him joy.
TRANIO
     Ay, and he'll tame her.
BIANCA   He says so, Tranio.
TRANIO
     Faith, he is gone unto the taming school.
BIANCA
     The taming school? What, is there such a place?
TRANIO
     Ay, mistress, and Petruchio is the master,
     That teacheth tricks eleven and twenty long   57
     To tame a shrew and charm her chattering tongue.
          Enter Biondello.
BIONDELLO
     O master, master, I have watched so long
     That I am dog-weary, but at last I spied   60
     An ancient angel coming down the hill   61
     Will serve the turn.   62

---

48 *Tranio* (Lucentio has revealed Tranio's identity to Bianca in III.1.35)   50
lusty (1) merry, (2) lustful   57 *eleven . . . long* i.e., a great many (referring to
the card game of one-and-thirty)   61 *angel* fellow of the good old stamp (an
"angel" being a gold coin)   62 *the turn* our purposes

TRANIO   What is he, Biondello?

BIONDELLO

63   Master, a mercatante or a pedant,
      I know not what; but formal in apparel,
65   In gait and countenance surely like a father.

LUCENTIO
      And what of him, Tranio?

TRANIO

67   If he be credulous and trust my tale
      I'll make him glad to seem Vincentio,
      And give assurance to Baptista Minola
70   As if he were the right Vincentio.
      Take in your love and then let me alone.

                        [Exeunt Lucentio and Bianca.]

      Enter a Pedant.

PEDANT
      God save you, sir.

TRANIO   And you, sir. You are welcome.

73   Travel you far on, or are you at the farthest?

PEDANT
      Sir, at the farthest for a week or two,
75   But then up farther and as far as Rome,
      And so to Tripoli, if God lend me life.

TRANIO
      What countryman, I pray?

PEDANT   Of Mantua.

TRANIO
      Of Mantua, sir? Marry, God forbid!
      And come to Padua, careless of your life?

PEDANT

80   My life, sir? How, I pray? For that goes hard.

---

63 *mercatante* merchant; *pedant* schoolmaster 65 *countenance* appearance
67 *trust my tale* believe what I tell him 73 *far on* farther; *at the farthest* i.e.,
at your destination 75–76 *up . . . Tripoli* (Padua is "up" from Mantua, but
Rome is very far south; Tripoli is either the North African city and state or
the city in Syria) 80 *goes hard* is serious

TRANIO

'Tis death for anyone in Mantua
To come to Padua. Know you not the cause?
Your ships are stayed at Venice, and the duke – 83
For private quarrel 'twixt your duke and him –
Hath published and proclaimed it openly.
'Tis marvel, but that you are newly come, 86
You might have heard it else proclaimed about.

PEDANT

Alas, sir, it is worse for me than so,
For I have bills for money by exchange
From Florence and must here deliver them. 89
90

TRANIO

Well, sir, to do you courtesy, 91
This will I do and thus I will advise you –
First, tell me, have you ever been at Pisa?

PEDANT

Ay, sir, in Pisa have I often been,
Pisa, renownèd for grave citizens.

TRANIO

Among them, know you one Vincentio?

PEDANT

I know him not but I have heard of him,
A merchant of incomparable wealth.

TRANIO

He is my father, sir, and sooth to say,
In count'nance somewhat doth resemble you. 100

BIONDELLO   *[Aside]* As much as an apple doth an oyster,
and all one. 102

TRANIO

To save your life in this extremity
This favor will I do you for his sake,
And think it not the worst of all your fortunes

---

83 *stayed* impounded   86 *but that* except for the fact that   89 *bills . . . exchange* (bills of exchange were money orders due on a certain date)   91 *courtesy* a good turn   102 *all one* no matter

That you are like to Sir Vincentio.
107   His name and credit shall you undertake,
And in my house you shall be friendly lodged.
109   Look that you take upon you as you should.
110   You understand me, sir. So shall you stay
Till you have done your business in the city.
If this be courtesy, sir, accept of it.

PEDANT
113   O sir, I do, and will repute you ever
The patron of my life and liberty.

TRANIO
Then go with me to make the matter good.
116   This, by the way, I let you understand.
My father is here looked for every day
118   To pass assurance of a dower in marriage
'Twixt me and one Baptista's daughter here.
120   In all these circumstances I'll instruct you.
Go with me to clothe you as becomes you.   *Exeunt.*

*

⌒ **IV.3** *Enter Kate and Grumio.*

GRUMIO
No, no, forsooth, I dare not for my life.

KATE
2   The more my wrong, the more his spite appears.
What, did he marry me to famish me?
Beggars that come unto my father's door,
5   Upon entreaty have a present alms;
If not, elsewhere they meet with charity.
But I, who never knew how to entreat
Nor never needed that I should entreat,

---

107 *credit* reputation; *undertake* assume   109 *take upon you* play your part
113 *repute* consider   116 *by the way* along the way, as we go   118 *pass* convey (legal term); *assurance* a guarantee
    IV.3 Petruchio's house   2 *my wrong* i.e., the wrong done me   5 *a present* immediate

Am starved for meat, giddy for lack of sleep,   9
With oaths kept waking and with brawling fed.   10
And that which spites me more than all these wants,
He does it under name of perfect love,
As who should say, if I should sleep or eat   13
'Twere deadly sickness or else present death.
I prithee go and get me some repast,
I care not what, so it be wholesome food.

GRUMIO
What say you to a neat's foot?   17

KATE
'Tis passing good, I prithee let me have it.

GRUMIO
I fear it is too choleric a meat.   19
How say you to a fat tripe finely broiled?   20

KATE
I like it well, good Grumio, fetch it me.

GRUMIO
I cannot tell; I fear 'tis choleric.
What say you to a piece of beef and mustard?

KATE
A dish that I do love to feed upon.

GRUMIO
Ay, but the mustard is too hot a little.

KATE
Why then, the beef, and let the mustard rest.

GRUMIO
Nay then, I will not; you shall have the mustard
Or else you get no beef of Grumio.

KATE
Then both or one, or anything thou wilt.

GRUMIO
Why then, the mustard without the beef.   30

---

9 *meat* food   13 *As who* as though one   17 *a neat's foot* an ox's or a calf's foot
19 *choleric* engendering anger

KATE

    Go, get thee gone, thou false deluding slave,
      Beats him.

32   That feed'st me with the very name of meat.
    Sorrow on thee and all the pack of you
    That triumph thus upon my misery.
    Go, get thee gone, I say.
      Enter Petruchio and Hortensio with meat.

PETRUCHIO

36   How fares my Kate? What, sweeting, all amort?

HORTENSIO

    Mistress, what cheer?

KATE   Faith, as cold as can be.

PETRUCHIO

    Pluck up thy spirits, look cheerfully upon me.
    Here, love, thou seest how diligent I am

40   To dress thy meat myself and bring it thee.
    I am sure, sweet Kate, this kindness merits thanks.
    What, not a word? Nay then, thou lov'st it not,

43   And all my pains is sorted to no proof.
    Here, take away this dish.

KATE   I pray you, let it stand.

PETRUCHIO

    The poorest service is repaid with thanks,
    And so shall mine before you touch the meat.

KATE

    I thank you, sir.

HORTENSIO

    Signor Petruchio, fie, you are to blame.
    Come, Mistress Kate, I'll bear you company.
      [They sit at table.]

PETRUCHIO   *[Aside]*

50   Eat it up all, Hortensio, if thou lov'st me.
    Much good of it unto thy gentle heart.

---

32 *very* i.e., mere   36 *sweeting* sweetheart; *all amort* spiritless, dejected   **40**
dress prepare   43 *is . . . proof* have resulted in nothing

Kate, eat apace. And now, my honey love,   52
Will we return unto thy father's house
And revel it as bravely as the best,   54
With silken coats and caps and golden rings,
With ruffs and cuffs and farthingales and things;   56
With scarfs and fans and double change of bravery,   57
With amber bracelets, beads, and all this knavery.
What, hast thou dined? The tailor stays thy leisure,
To deck thy body with his ruffling treasure.   60
    Enter Tailor [with a gown].
Come, tailor, let us see these ornaments.
    Enter Haberdasher [with a cap].
Lay forth the gown. – What news with you, sir?

HABERDASHER
Here is the cap your worship did bespeak.   63

PETRUCHIO
Why, this was molded on a porringer: 64
A velvet dish. Fie, fie, 'tis lewd and filthy.   65
Why, 'tis a cockle or a walnut shell,   66
A knack, a toy, a trick, a baby's cap.   67
Away with it. Come, let me have a bigger.

KATE
I'll have no bigger, this doth fit the time,   69
And gentlewomen wear such caps as these.   70

PETRUCHIO
When you are gentle you shall have one too,
And not till then.

HORTENSIO   That will not be in haste.

KATE
Why, sir, I trust I may have leave to speak,
And speak I will. I am no child, no babe.
Your betters have endured me say my mind,   75

---

52 *apace* quickly   54 *bravely* finely dressed   56 *farthingales* hooped petti-
coats   57 *bravery* finery   60 *ruffling* ornamented with ruffles   63 *bespeak*
order   64 *porringer* porridge bowl   65 *lewd* vile   66 *cockle* cockleshell   67
knack trinket; *trick* trifle   69 *fit the time* accord with present fashion   75 *say*
speaking

And if you cannot, best you stop your ears.
My tongue will tell the anger of my heart
Or else my heart, concealing it, will break,
And rather than it shall, I will be free
80 Even to the uttermost, as I please, in words.

PETRUCHIO
Why, thou sayst true. It is a paltry cap,
82 A custard coffin, a bauble, a silken pie.
I love thee well in that thou lik'st it not.

KATE
Love me or love me not, I like the cap,
And I will have it or I will have none.

                              [Exit Haberdasher.]

PETRUCHIO
Thy gown? Why, ay – come, tailor, let us see't.
87 O mercy, God, what masquing stuff is here?
88 What's this, a sleeve? 'Tis like a demicannon.
89 What, up and down carved like an apple tart?
90 Here's snip and nip and cut and slish and slash,
91 Like to a censer in a barber's shop.
Why, what a devil's name, tailor, call'st thou this?

HORTENSIO   *[Aside]*
I see she's like to have neither cap nor gown.

TAILOR
You bid me make it orderly and well,
According to the fashion and the time.

PETRUCHIO
Marry, I did. But if you be remembered,
I did not bid you mar it to the time.
98 Go, hop me over every kennel home,
For you shall hop without my custom, sir.

---

82 *custard coffin* crust of a custard pie; *silken pie* pie of silk   87 *masquing stuff* clothing fit for masquerades   88 *demicannon* large cannon   89 *carved . . . tart* (the sleeve has slashes, like the slits in a piecrust, to show the fabric beneath)   91 *censer* incense burner (with perforated cover)   98 *hop . . . home* you can hop home over every gutter for all I care

I'll none of it. Hence, make your best of it.   *100*
KATE
   I never saw a better-fashioned gown,
   More quaint, more pleasing, nor more commendable.   *102*
   Belike you mean to make a puppet of me.   *103*
PETRUCHIO
   Why, true, he means to make a puppet of thee.
TAILOR
   She says your worship means to make a puppet of her.
PETRUCHIO
   O monstrous arrogance!
   Thou liest, thou thread, thou thimble,
   Thou yard, three-quarters, half-yard, quarter, nail!   *108*
   Thou flea, thou nit, thou winter cricket thou!   *109*
   Braved in mine own house with a skein of thread?   *110*
   Away, thou rag, thou quantity, thou remnant,   *111*
   Or I shall so bemete thee with thy yard   *112*
   As thou shalt think on prating whilst thou liv'st.   *113*
   I tell thee, I, that thou hast marred her gown.
TAILOR
   Your worship is deceived. The gown is made
   Just as my master had direction.
   Grumio gave order how it should be done.
GRUMIO   I gave him no order, I gave him the stuff.   *118*
TAILOR
   But how did you desire it should be made?
GRUMIO   Marry, sir, with needle and thread.   *120*
TAILOR
   But did you not request to have it cut?
GRUMIO   Thou hast faced many things.   *122*
TAILOR   I have.

---

102 *quaint* elegant   103 *Belike* it seems; *puppet* (contemptuous term for a woman)   108 *nail* two and a quarter inches (a measure of length for cloth)   109 *nit* louse egg   110 *Braved* defied; *with* by   111 *quantity* fragment   112 *bemete* punish; *yard* yardstick   113 *think on* think before   118 *stuff* cloth   122 *faced* (1) trimmed, (2) faced down

124 GRUMIO Face not me. Thou hast braved many men:
brave not me. I will neither be faced nor braved. I say
unto thee, I bid thy master cut out the gown but I did
127 not bid him cut it to pieces. Ergo, thou liest.

128 TAILOR Why, here is the note of the fashion to testify.

PETRUCHIO Read it.

130 GRUMIO The note lies in's throat if he say I said so.

131 TAILOR [Reads.] "Imprimis, a loose-bodied gown –"

GRUMIO Master, if ever I said loose-bodied gown, sew
133 me in the skirts of it and beat me to death with a bottom of brown thread. I said, a gown.

PETRUCHIO Proceed.

136 TAILOR "With a small compassed cape –"

GRUMIO I confess the cape.

138 TAILOR "With a trunk sleeve –"

GRUMIO I confess two sleeves.

140 TAILOR "The sleeves curiously cut."

PETRUCHIO Ay, there's the villainy.

GRUMIO Error i' th' bill, sir, error i' th' bill. I commanded the sleeves should be cut out and sewed up
144 again, and that I'll prove upon thee, though thy little
finger be armed in a thimble.

146 TAILOR This is true that I say. An I had thee in place
where thou shouldst know it.

148 GRUMIO I am for thee straight. Take thou the bill, give
149 me thy meteyard, and spare not me.

150 HORTENSIO God-a-mercy, Grumio, then he shall have
no odds.

---

124 *braved* (1) dressed finely, (2) defied 127 *Ergo* therefore (Latin) 128 *to
testify* as evidence 130 *lies . . . throat* (1) is a low (musical) note, (2) is an
outrageous lie 131 *Imprimis* first; *loose-bodied gown* (Loose gowns were
fashionable; all editors claim that the point is that prostitutes wore them, but
they wore them because fashionable ladies wore them. The point is that there
is nothing wrong with the dress.) 133–34 *bottom* skein 136 *compassed*
flared 138 *trunk* very full 140 *curiously* elaborately 144 *prove upon thee*
maintain by defeating you in combat 146–47 *An . . . where* if only I had
you in the right place 148 *bill* (punning on the weapon: a bill was a hal-
berd) 149 *meteyard* yardstick 150–51 *he . . . odds* he won't have a chance

PETRUCHIO   Well, sir, in brief, the gown is not for me.

GRUMIO   You are i' th' right, sir, 'tis for my mistress.

PETRUCHIO   Go, take it up unto thy master's use.   154

GRUMIO   Villain, not for thy life. Take up my mistress'   155
gown for thy master's use!

PETRUCHIO   Why, sir, what's your conceit in that?   157

GRUMIO

O sir, the conceit is deeper than you think for.
Take up my mistress' gown to his master's use!
O fie, fie, fie!   160

PETRUCHIO   *[Aside]*

Hortensio, say thou wilt see the tailor paid.
[To Tailor]
Go take it hence, be gone and say no more.

HORTENSIO

Tailor, I'll pay thee for thy gown tomorrow.
Take no unkindness of his hasty words.
Away, I say. Commend me to thy master.   *Exit Tailor.*

PETRUCHIO

Well, come, my Kate; we will unto your father's,
Even in these honest mean habiliments.   167
Our purses shall be proud, our garments poor,
For 'tis the mind that makes the body rich;
And as the sun breaks through the darkest clouds   170
So honor peereth in the meanest habit.   171
What, is the jay more precious than the lark
Because his feathers are more beautiful?
Or is the adder better than the eel
Because his painted skin contents the eye?
O no, good Kate; neither art thou the worse
For this poor furniture and mean array.   177
If thou account'st it shame, lay it on me.   178

---

154 *take . . . use* i.e., return it to your master for whatever use he can make of
it 155–56 *Take . . . gown* i.e., lift up her skirts 157 *conceit* meaning 167
honest . . . habiliments respectable, plain clothes 171 *peereth in* appears
through; *habit* clothing 177 *furniture* clothing 178 *lay it* blame it

179   And therefore frolic; we will hence forthwith
180   To feast and sport us at thy father's house.
          [To Grumio]
       Go call my men, and let us straight to him;
       And bring our horses unto Long Lane end.
       There will we mount, and thither walk on foot.
       Let's see, I think 'tis now some seven o'clock,
185   And well we may come there by dinnertime.

KATE
       I dare assure you, sir, 'tis almost two,
       And 'twill be suppertime ere you come there.

PETRUCHIO
       It shall be seven ere I go to horse.
189   Look what I speak or do or think to do,
190   You are still crossing it. Sirs, let't alone.
       I will not go today, and ere I do,
       It shall be what o'clock I say it is.

HORTENSIO
       Why, so this gallant will command the sun.   *[Exeunt.]*

                              *

∾ **IV.4** *Enter Tranio [as Lucentio] and the Pedant
          booted and dressed like Vincentio.*

TRANIO
       Sir, this is the house. Please it you that I call?
PEDANT
2   Ay, what else? And but I be deceived,
3   Signor Baptista may remember me,
       Near twenty years ago, in Genoa,
5   Where we were lodgers at the Pegasus.

---

179 *hence* i.e., go hence; *forthwith* immediately   185 *dinnertime* about noon
189 *Look what* whatever
    IV.4 Before Baptista's house   s.d. *booted* (as from traveling)   2 *but* un-
less   3 *may remember me* (the pedant is rehearsing his part)   5 *Pegasus*
(name of an inn, after the winged horse of classical myth)

TRANIO

    'Tis well, and hold your own in any case

    With such austerity as longeth to a father.   7

    Enter Biondello.

PEDANT

    I warrant you. But sir, here comes your boy;

    'Twere good he were schooled.   9

TRANIO

    Fear you not him. Sirrah Biondello,   *10*

    Now do your duty throughly, I advise you.   11

    Imagine 'twere the right Vincentio.

BIONDELLO

    Tut, fear not me.

TRANIO

    But hast thou done thy errand to Baptista?

BIONDELLO

    I told him that your father was at Venice,

    And that you looked for him this day in Padua.   16

TRANIO

    Thou'rt a tall fellow. Hold thee that to drink.   17

    [Gives money.]

    Here comes Baptista. Set your countenance, sir.   18

    Enter Baptista and Lucentio [as Cambio]. Pedant

    bareheaded.

    Signor Baptista, you are happily met.

    [To Pedant]

    Sir, this is the gentleman I told you of.   *20*

    I pray you, stand good father to me now,   21

    Give me Bianca for my patrimony.

PEDANT

    Soft, son.

    Sir, by your leave. Having come to Padua

---

7 *austerity* dignity; *longeth to* befits   9 *schooled* taught how to play his part
11 *throughly* thoroughly   16 *looked for* expected   17 *tall* fine; *Hold . . .
drink* have a drink on me   18 *Set . . . countenance* i.e., look dignified;
s.d. *bareheaded* (the pedant doffs his hat to Baptista)   21 *stand* prove to be a

To gather in some debts, my son Lucentio
Made me acquainted with a weighty cause
Of love between your daughter and himself.
And – for the good report I hear of you,
And for the love he beareth to your daughter,
30 And she to him – to stay him not too long,
I am content, in a good father's care,
32 To have him matched. And if you please to like
No worse than I, upon some agreement
Me shall you find ready and willing
35 With one consent to have her so bestowed.
36 For curious I cannot be with you,
Signor Baptista, of whom I hear so well.

BAPTISTA
Sir, pardon me in what I have to say.
Your plainness and your shortness please me well.
40 Right true it is, your son Lucentio here
Doth love my daughter, and she loveth him –
Or both dissemble deeply their affections.
And therefore if you say no more than this,
That like a father you will deal with him
45 And pass my daughter a sufficient dower,
The match is made and all is done:
Your son shall have my daughter with consent.

TRANIO
I thank you, sir. Where then do you know best
49 We be affied and such assurance ta'en
50 As shall with either part's agreement stand?

BAPTISTA
Not in my house, Lucentio, for you know
Pitchers have ears, and I have many servants.

---

30 *stay* delay 32 *like* approve (the match) 35 *With . . . consent* i.e., with
the same consent as yours 36 *curious* overparticular, fussy 45 *pass* settle on
49 *affied* formally betrothed 49–50 *such . . . stand* such guarantees be given
as shall formalize our agreement

Besides, old Gremio is hearkening still,   53
And happily we might be interrupted.   54

TRANIO

Then at my lodging, an it like you.   55
There doth my father lie, and there this night   56
We'll pass the business privately and well.   57
Send for your daughter by your servant here.
My boy shall fetch the scrivener presently.   59
The worst is this, that at so slender warning   60
You are like to have a thin and slender pittance.   61

BAPTISTA

It likes me well. Cambio, hie you home   62
And bid Bianca make her ready straight.
And if you will, tell what hath happenèd:
Lucentio's father is arrived in Padua,
And how she's like to be Lucentio's wife.

                                        [Exit Lucentio.]

BIONDELLO

I pray the gods she may with all my heart.   Exit.

TRANIO

Dally not with the gods, but get thee gone.
Signor Baptista, shall I lead the way?
Welcome, one mess is like to be your cheer.   70
Come, sir, we will better it in Pisa.

BAPTISTA   I follow you.   Exeunt.

    Enter [severally] Lucentio [as Cambio] and Biondello.

BIONDELLO   Cambio!

LUCENTIO   What sayst thou, Biondello?

BIONDELLO   You saw my master wink and laugh upon
you?

LUCENTIO   Biondello, what of that?

---

53 *hearkening still* always eavesdropping 54 *happily* perhaps 55 *an . . .
you* if you please 56 *lie* lodge 57 *pass* transact 59 *scrivener* notary (a
scribe empowered to draw up legal agreements) 61 *pittance* meal 62 *likes
me* pleases me 70 *mess* dish; *cheer* entertainment

BIONDELLO   Faith, nothing, but he's left me here behind
79   to expound the meaning or moral of his signs and to-
80   kens.
81 LUCENTIO   I pray thee, moralize them.
82 BIONDELLO   Then thus. Baptista is safe, talking with the
        deceiving father of a deceitful son.
    LUCENTIO   And what of him?
    BIONDELLO   His daughter is to be brought by you to the
        supper.
    LUCENTIO   And then?
    BIONDELLO   The old priest at Saint Luke's church is at
        your command at all hours.
90 LUCENTIO   And what of all this?
    BIONDELLO   I cannot tell, except they are busied about a
92   counterfeit assurance. Take you assurance of her, "cum
        privilegio ad imprimendum solum." To th' church with
        the priest, clerk, and some sufficient honest witnesses.
        If this be not that you look for, I have no more to say,
        But bid Bianca farewell forever and a day.
    LUCENTIO   Hear'st thou, Biondello –
    BIONDELLO   I cannot tarry. I knew a wench married in an
        afternoon as she went to the garden for parsley to stuff a
100   rabbit, and so may you, sir, and so adieu, sir. My master
        hath appointed me to go to Saint Luke's, to bid the
102   priest be ready against you come with your appendix.
                                                    Exit.

LUCENTIO
    I may and will, if she be so contented.
    She will be pleased, then wherefore should I doubt?

---

79 *moral* deep significance   81 *moralize* explain   82 *safe* i.e., safely dealt
with   92 *assurance* agreement (the betrothal); *Take . . . assurance* insure
yourself (by marrying her)   92–93 *cum . . . solum* with exclusive right to
print (Latin; the publisher's copyright formula, analogized to the husband's
exclusive right to "imprint himself on" his wife)   102 *against . . . come* in anticipation of your coming; *appendix* appendage (i.e., bride)

Hap what hap may, I'll roundly go about her.   105
It shall go hard if Cambio go without her.   *Exit.* 106

                          ✳

❧ **IV.5** *Enter Petruchio, Kate, Hortensio [, and Grumio,
with Attendants].*

PETRUCHIO
Come on, a God's name, once more toward our father's. 1
Good Lord, how bright and goodly shines the moon!
KATE
The moon? The sun. It is not moonlight now.
PETRUCHIO
I say it is the moon that shines so bright.
KATE
I know it is the sun that shines so bright.
PETRUCHIO
Now by my mother's son, and that's myself,
It shall be moon or star or what I list,   7
Or e'er I journey to your father's house.   8
    [To Servants]
Go on and fetch our horses back again.
Evermore crossed and crossed, nothing but crossed.   10
HORTENSIO   *[Aside to Kate]*
Say as he says or we shall never go.
KATE
Forward, I pray, since we have come so far,
And be it moon or sun or what you please.
An if you please to call it a rush candle,   14
Henceforth I vow it shall be so for me.
PETRUCHIO
I say it is the moon.
KATE   I know it is the moon.

──────────

105 *Hap . . . may* whatever comes of it; *I'll . . . her* I'll go find her immediately 106 *go hard* be hard to bear; *go* return
    IV.5 A country road 1 *a* in 7 *list* please 8 *Or* ere, before 14 *rush
candle* rush dipped in grease to serve as candle

PETRUCHIO

    Nay, then you lie. It is the blessèd sun.

KATE

    Then God be blessed, it is the blessèd sun,

    But sun it is not when you say it is not,

20   And the moon changes even as your mind.

    What you will have it named, even that it is,

22   And so it shall be still for Katherine.

HORTENSIO

    Petruchio, go thy ways, the field is won.

PETRUCHIO

24   Well, forward, forward! Thus the bowl should run,

25   And not unluckily against the bias.

    But soft, what company is coming here?

       Enter Vincentio.

       [To Vincentio]

    Good morrow, gentle mistress, where away?

    Tell me, sweet Kate, and tell me truly too,

    Hast thou beheld a fresher gentlewoman?

30   Such war of white and red within her cheeks!

    What stars do spangle heaven with such beauty

    As those two eyes become that heavenly face?

    Fair lovely maid, once more good day to thee.

    Sweet Kate, embrace her for her beauty's sake.

HORTENSIO   *[Aside]*

35   A will make the man mad, to make a woman of him.

KATE

    Young budding virgin, fair and fresh and sweet,

    Whither away, or where is thy abode?

    Happy the parents of so fair a child,

    Happier the man whom favorable stars

40   Allots thee for his lovely bedfellow.

---

22 *still* always   24 *bowl* ball in game of bowls   25 *unluckily* unsuccessfully; *against the bias* contrary to the intended course (the bias being a weight in the side of the bowl that enables the bowler to roll it in a curve)   35 *A* he

PETRUCHIO

   Why, how now, Kate, I hope thou art not mad.
   This is a man, old, wrinkled, faded, withered,
   And not a maiden, as thou sayst he is.

KATE

   Pardon, old father, my mistaking eyes   44
   That have been so bedazzled with the sun
   That everything I look on seemeth green.   46
   Now I perceive thou art a reverend father.
   Pardon, I pray thee, for my mad mistaking.

PETRUCHIO

   Do, good old grandsire, and withal make known
   Which way thou travelest. If along with us,   50
   We shall be joyful of thy company.

VINCENTIO

   Fair sir, and you my merry mistress,
   That with your strange encounter much amazed me, 53
   My name is called Vincentio, my dwelling Pisa,
   And bound I am to Padua, there to visit
   A son of mine, which long I have not seen.

PETRUCHIO

   What is his name?

VINCENTIO   Lucentio, gentle sir.

PETRUCHIO

   Happily met, the happier for thy son.
   And now by law, as well as reverend age,
   I may entitle thee my loving father.   60
   The sister to my wife, this gentlewoman,
   Thy son by this hath married. Wonder not   62
   Nor be not grieved. She is of good esteem,   63
   Her dowry wealthy, and of worthy birth;

---

44 *father* (respectful term of address to an old man) 46 *green* young 53 *en-counter* greeting 62 *Thy . . . married* (since Petruchio has been out of town, he should not know this information, and in any case, Lucentio and Bianca are not married yet; moreover, Hortensio has heard the suitor he knows as Lucentio forswear her); *this* this time 63 *esteem* reputation

65 Beside, so qualified as may beseem
The spouse of any noble gentleman.
Let me embrace with old Vincentio,
68 And wander we to see thy honest son,
Who will of thy arrival be full joyous.

VINCENTIO
70 But is this true, or is it else your pleasure,
71 Like pleasant travelers, to break a jest
Upon the company you overtake?

HORTENSIO
I do assure thee, father, so it is.

PETRUCHIO
Come, go along, and see the truth hereof,
75 For our first merriment hath made thee jealous.

Exeunt [all but Hortensio].

HORTENSIO
Well, Petruchio, this has put me in heart.
77 Have to my widow, and if she be froward,
78 Then hast thou taught Hortensio to be untoward.

Exit.

*

∾ V.1 *Enter Biondello, Lucentio [as Cambio], and*
Bianca. Gremio is out before [and stands aside].

BIONDELLO   Softly and swiftly, sir, for the priest is ready.
LUCENTIO   I fly, Biondello – but they may chance to
need thee at home; therefore leave us.

Exit [with Bianca].

---

65 *so qualified* having such qualities   68 *wander we* let's go out of our way
71 *pleasant* merry   71–72 *break . . . / Upon* play a joke on   75 *jealous* suspicious   77 *froward* stubborn   78 *untoward* perverse, difficult (and thereby
how to tame her)

V.1 Before Lucentio's house   **s.d.** *out before* onstage before the others
(whom he does not "see")

BIONDELLO   Nay, faith, I'll see the church a your back,   4
and then come back to my master as soon as I can.

[Exit.]

GREMIO
  I marvel Cambio comes not all this while.
      Enter Petruchio, Kate, Vincentio, [and] Grumio, with
      Attendants.

PETRUCHIO
  Sir, here's the door, this is Lucentio's house.
  My father's bears more toward the marketplace.   8
  Thither must I, and here I leave you, sir.

VINCENTIO
  You shall not choose but drink before you go.   10
  I think I shall command your welcome here,
  And by all likelihood some cheer is toward.
      Knock.

GREMIO   *[Advancing]* They're busy within; you were best
knock louder.   14

      Pedant [as Vincentio] looks out of the window.

PEDANT   What's he that knocks as he would beat down   15
the gate?

VINCENTIO   Is Signor Lucentio within, sir?

PEDANT   He's within, sir, but not to be spoken withal.   18

VINCENTIO   What if a man bring him a hundred pound
or two, to make merry withal?   20

PEDANT   Keep your hundred pounds to yourself. He
shall need none so long as I live.

PETRUCHIO   Nay, I told you your son was well beloved in
Padua. Do you hear, sir? To leave frivolous circumstances, I pray you tell Signor Lucentio that his father is
come from Pisa and is here at the door to speak with
him.

---

4 *a your back* at your back (i.e., I'll see you enter it)   8 *bears* lies   14 s.d.
looks . . . window i.e., appears in the gallery over the stage – are Sly, the lord,
and his retinue still there?   15 *What* who   18 *withal* with

PEDANT   Thou liest. His father is come from Pisa and is
here looking out at the window.

30 VINCENTIO   Art thou his father?

PEDANT   Ay sir, so his mother says, if I may believe her.

PETRUCHIO   *[To Vincentio]* Why how now, gentleman!
33   Why this is flat knavery, to take upon you another
man's name.

PEDANT   Lay hands on the villain. I believe a means to
36   cozen somebody in this city under my countenance.

Enter Biondello.

BIONDELLO   I have seen them in the church together.
38   God send 'em good shipping! But who is here? Mine
39   old master, Vincentio! Now we are undone and
40   brought to nothing.

41 VINCENTIO   Come hither, crackhemp.

42 BIONDELLO   I hope I may choose, sir.

VINCENTIO   Come hither, you rogue. What, have you
forgot me?

BIONDELLO   Forgot you? No sir. I could not forget you,
for I never saw you before in all my life.

VINCENTIO   What, you notorious villain, didst thou
never see thy master's father, Vincentio?

BIONDELLO   What, my worshipful old master? Yes,
50   marry, sir, see where he looks out of the window.

VINCENTIO   Is't so indeed?

He beats Biondello.

BIONDELLO   Help, help, help! Here's a madman will
murder me.   *[Exit.]*

PEDANT   Help, son! Help, Signor Baptista! *[Exit above.]*

PETRUCHIO   Prithee, Kate, let's stand aside and see the
end of this controversy.

[They stand aside.]

---

33 *flat* downright   36 *cozen* cheat; *under my countenance* by posing as me
38 *good shipping* fair sailing   39 *undone* ruined   41 *crackhemp* fellow ripe
for hanging   42 *choose* do as I choose

Enter [below] Pedant [as Vincentio] with Servants,
Baptista, [and] Tranio [as Lucentio].

TRANIO   Sir, what are you that offer to beat my servant?   57

VINCENTIO   What am I, sir? Nay, what are you, sir? O immortal gods! O fine villain! A silken doublet, a velvet hose, a scarlet cloak, and a copatain hat! O I am undone,   60
I am undone! While I play the good husband at home,   61
my son and my servants spend all at the university.

TRANIO   How now, what's the matter?

BAPTISTA   What, is the man lunatic?

TRANIO   Sir, you seem a sober ancient gentleman by your habit, but your words show you a madman. Why sir,   66
what 'cerns it you if I wear pearl and gold? I thank my   67
good father, I am able to maintain it.

VINCENTIO   Thy father! O villain, he is a sailmaker in Bergamo.
   70

BAPTISTA   You mistake, sir, you mistake, sir. Pray, what do you think is his name?

VINCENTIO   His name? As if I knew not his name! I have brought him up ever since he was three years old, and his name is Tranio.

PEDANT   Away, away, mad ass! His name is Lucentio. He is mine only son, and heir to the lands of me, Signor Vincentio.

VINCENTIO   Lucentio? O he hath murdered his master! Lay hold on him, I charge you in the duke's name. O   80
my son, my son! Tell me, thou villain, where is my son Lucentio?

TRANIO   *[To a Servant]* Call forth an officer.
     [Enter an Officer.]
Carry this mad knave to the jail. Father Baptista, I charge you see that he be forthcoming.
   85

VINCENTIO   Carry me to the jail!

---

57 *what* who   60 *copatain* high-crowned   61 *good husband* careful manager
66 *habit* bearing   67 *'cerns* concerns   70 *Bergamo* (like Mantua and Padua, not a seaport)   85 *forthcoming* i.e., to stand trial

GREMIO   Stay, officer, he shall not go to prison.

BAPTISTA   Talk not, Signor Gremio. I say he shall go to prison.

90   GREMIO   Take heed, Signor Baptista, lest you be cony-catched in this business. I dare swear this is the right Vincentio.

PEDANT   Swear, if thou dar'st.

GREMIO   Nay, I dare not swear it.

95   TRANIO   Then thou wert best say that I am not Lucentio.

GREMIO   Yes, I know thee to be Signor Lucentio.

BAPTISTA   Away with the dotard, to the jail with him!

Enter Biondello, Lucentio, and Bianca.

98   VINCENTIO   Thus strangers may be halèd and abused. O monstrous villain!

100   BIONDELLO   O we are spoiled, yonder he is. Deny him, forswear him, or else we are all undone.

*Exeunt Biondello, Tranio, and Pedant
as fast as may be.*

LUCENTIO   Pardon, sweet father.

Kneel.

VINCENTIO   Lives my sweet son?

BIANCA   Pardon, dear father.

BAPTISTA

How hast thou offended? Where is Lucentio?

LUCENTIO

Here's Lucentio, right son to the right Vincentio,
That have by marriage made thy daughter mine
108   While counterfeit supposes bleared thine eyne.

GREMIO

109   Here's packing, with a witness, to deceive us all!

VINCENTIO

110   Where is that damnèd villain Tranio,

90–91 *cony-catched* duped 95 *wert best* might as well 98 *halèd* hauled about, molested 108 *counterfeit supposes* false assumptions (with an allusion to Gascoigne's play *Supposes*); *eyne* eyes 109 *packing* plotting; *with a witness* with a vengeance

That faced and braved me in this matter so?   111

BAPTISTA
Why, tell me, is not this my Cambio?

BIANCA
Cambio is changed into Lucentio.

LUCENTIO
Love wrought these miracles. Bianca's love
Made me exchange my state with Tranio
While he did bear my countenance in the town,   116
And happily I have arrived at the last
Unto the wished haven of my bliss.
What Tranio did, myself enforced him to;
Then pardon him, sweet father, for my sake.   120

VINCENTIO   I'll slit the villain's nose that would have sent
me to the jail.

BAPTISTA   *[To Lucentio]* But do you hear, sir? Have you
married my daughter without asking my good will?

VINCENTIO   Fear not, Baptista, we will content you, go   125
to. But I will in, to be revenged for this villainy.   *Exit.*

BAPTISTA   And I, to sound the depth of this knavery.
                                                  Exit.

LUCENTIO   Look not pale, Bianca, thy father will not
frown.   *Exeunt [Lucentio and Bianca].*

GREMIO
My cake is dough, but I'll in among the rest,   130
Out of hope of all but my share of the feast.   *[Exit.]*

KATE   *[Advancing]* Husband, let's follow, to see the end
of this ado.

PETRUCHIO   First kiss me, Kate, and we will.

KATE   What, in the midst of the street?

PETRUCHIO   What, art thou ashamed of me?

KATE   No sir, God forbid, but ashamed to kiss.

---

111 *faced and braved* outfaced and defied   116 *bear my countenance* pose as
me   125–26 *go to* (expression of impatience)   130 *My cake is dough* i.e., my
hopes are dashed (proverbial)

PETRUCHIO

   Why, then let's home again.
     [To Grumio]   Come, sirrah, let's away.

KATE

   Nay, I will give thee a kiss. Now pray thee, love, stay.

PETRUCHIO

140   Is not this well? Come, my sweet Kate.

141   Better once than never, for never's too late.   *Exeunt.*

*

  ～ **V.2** *Enter Baptista, Vincentio, Gremio, the Pedant,*
    Lucentio, and Bianca; Tranio, Biondello, [and]
    Grumio; [Petruchio, Kate, Hortensio,] and Widow;
    the Servingmen with Tranio bringing in a banquet.

LUCENTIO

1   At last, though long, our jarring notes agree,
   And time it is, when raging war is done,
   To smile at scapes and perils overblown.
   My fair Bianca, bid my father welcome
   While I with selfsame kindness welcome thine.
   Brother Petruchio, sister Katherina,
   And thou, Hortensio, with thy loving widow,
   Feast with the best and welcome to my house.
   My banquet is to close our stomachs up
10 After our great good cheer. Pray you, sit down,
   For now we sit to chat as well as eat.
    [They sit at table.]

PETRUCHIO

   Nothing but sit and sit, and eat and eat!

BAPTISTA

   Padua affords this kindness, son Petruchio.

---

141 *Better . . . late* i.e., better late than never (proverbial); *once* at one time or another
   V.2 Lucentio's house **s.d.** *bringing in* i.e., carrying onstage; *banquet* dessert (sweets, fruit, and wine) 1 *long* after a long time 10 *After . . . cheer* (Lucentio's banquet apparently follows a bridal feast given by Baptista)

PETRUCHIO
   Padua affords nothing but what is kind.
HORTENSIO
   For both our sakes I would that word were true.
PETRUCHIO
   Now, for my life, Hortensio fears his widow.   16
WIDOW
   Then never trust me if I be afeard.   17
PETRUCHIO
   You are very sensible, and yet you miss my sense:
   I mean Hortensio is afeard of you.
WIDOW
   He that is giddy thinks the world turns round.   20
PETRUCHIO
   Roundly replied.   21
KATE   Mistress, how mean you that?
WIDOW
   Thus I conceive by him.   22
PETRUCHIO
   Conceive by me? How likes Hortensio that?
HORTENSIO
   My widow says, thus she conceives her tale.   24
PETRUCHIO
   Very well mended. Kiss him for that, good widow.
KATE
   "He that is giddy thinks the world turns round" –
   I pray you, tell me what you meant by that.
WIDOW
   Your husband, being troubled with a shrew,   28
   Measures my husband's sorrow by his woe –   29
   And now you know my meaning.   30

---

16 *fears* is afraid of (the widow quibbles on "frightens")   17 *afeard* fright-
ened (Petruchio quibbles on "suspicious")   21 *Roundly* straightforwardly
22 *conceive by* am inspired by (Petruchio quibbles on "become pregnant by")
24 *conceives* devises   28, 29 *shrew, woe* (a rhyme, as at IV.1.200–1)   29
Measures judges

KATE
31   A very mean meaning.
WIDOW   Right, I mean you.
KATE
32   And I am mean indeed, respecting you.
PETRUCHIO
     To her, Kate!
HORTENSIO
     To her, widow!
PETRUCHIO
35   A hundred marks, my Kate does put her down.
HORTENSIO
     That's my office.
PETRUCHIO
37   Spoke like an officer – ha' to thee, lad.
          Drinks to Hortensio.
BAPTISTA
     How likes Gremio these quick-witted folks?
GREMIO
     Believe me, sir, they butt together well.
BIANCA
40   Head and butt! An hasty-witted body
41   Would say your head and butt were head and horn.
VINCENTIO
     Ay, mistress bride, hath that awakened you?
BIANCA
     Ay, but not frighted me; therefore I'll sleep again.
PETRUCHIO
     Nay, that you shall not; since you have begun,
45   Have at you for a better jest or two.

---

31 *mean* contemptible (the widow quibbles on "have in mind," and Kate
then quibbles on "moderate" – i.e., in shrewishness)   32 *respecting* compared with   35 *put her down* defeat her (Hortensio quibbles on "have sex
with her")   37 *ha' to* here's to   40 *hasty-witted body* quick-witted person
41 *Would . . . horn* (presumably the usual joke about cuckoldry, but it is not
clear why this should be aimed at the unmarried Gremio)   45 *Have . . . for*
get ready for

BIANCA
    Am I your bird? I mean to shift my bush,
    And then pursue me as you draw your bow.
    You are welcome all.   48
                    Exit Bianca [with Kate and Widow].
PETRUCHIO
    She hath prevented me. Here, Signor Tranio,   49
    This bird you aimed at, though you hit her not.   50
    Therefore a health to all that shot and missed.
TRANIO
    O sir, Lucentio slipped me, like his greyhound,   52
    Which runs himself and catches for his master.
PETRUCHIO
    A good swift simile but something currish.
TRANIO
    'Tis well, sir, that you hunted for yourself;
    'Tis thought your deer does hold you at a bay.
BAPTISTA
    O ho, Petruchio! Tranio hits you now.
LUCENTIO
    I thank thee for that gird, good Tranio.   58
HORTENSIO
    Confess, confess, hath he not hit you here?
PETRUCHIO
    A has a little galled me, I confess,   60
    And as the jest did glance away from me,
    'Tis ten to one it maimed you two outright.
BAPTISTA
    Now, in good sadness, son Petruchio,   63
    I think thou hast the veriest shrew of all.   64
PETRUCHIO
    Well, I say no. And therefore, for assurance,   65

---

48 *You . . . all* (Bianca, as the hostess, leads the ladies out) 49 *prevented*
forestalled; *Signor* (Petruchio ironically addresses Tranio as a gentleman) 52
slipped unleashed 58 *gird* taunt 60 *A* he; *galled* annoyed 63 *sadness* seri-
ousness 64 *veriest* most perfect 65 *assurance* proof

Let's each one send unto his wife,
And he whose wife is most obedient,
To come at first when he doth send for her,
Shall win the wager which we will propose.

HORTENSIO
70   Content. What's the wager?

LUCENTIO   Twenty crowns.

PETRUCHIO
Twenty crowns?
72   I'll venture so much of my hawk or hound,
But twenty times so much upon my wife.

LUCENTIO
74   A hundred then.

HORTENSIO   Content.

PETRUCHIO   A match, 'tis done.

HORTENSIO
Who shall begin?

LUCENTIO
That will I.
Go, Biondello, bid your mistress come to me.

BIONDELLO   I go.   *Exit.*

BAPTISTA
79   Son, I'll be your half, Bianca comes.

LUCENTIO
80   I'll have no halves; I'll bear it all myself.
      Enter Biondello.
How now, what news?

BIONDELLO
Sir, my mistress sends you word
That she is busy and she cannot come.

PETRUCHIO
How? "She's busy and she cannot come"?
Is that an answer?

GREMIO   Ay, and a kind one too.
Pray God, sir, your wife send you not a worse.

---

72 *of* on   74 *match* bet   79 *be your half* take half your bet that

PETRUCHIO   I hope better.

HORTENSIO   Sirrah Biondello, go and entreat my wife to
come to me forthwith.   *Exit Biondello.*   89

PETRUCHIO   O ho, "entreat her"! Nay, then she must   90
needs come.

HORTENSIO   I am afraid, sir, do what you can, yours will
not be entreated. *(Enter Biondello.)* Now where's my
wife?

BIONDELLO

She says you have some goodly jest in hand.
She will not come. She bids you come to her.

PETRUCHIO

Worse and worse, "she will not come"!
O vile, intolerable, not to be endured!
Sirrah Grumio, go to your mistress,
Say I command her come to me.   *Exit [Grumio].*   100

HORTENSIO   I know her answer.

PETRUCHIO   What?

HORTENSIO   She will not.

PETRUCHIO

The fouler fortune mine, and there an end.
   Enter Kate [with Grumio].

BAPTISTA

Now, by my halidom, here comes Katherina!   105

KATE

What is your will, sir, that you send for me?

PETRUCHIO

Where is your sister and Hortensio's wife?

KATE

They sit conferring by the parlor fire.

PETRUCHIO

Go fetch them hither. If they deny to come,
Swinge me them soundly forth unto their husbands.   110

---

89 *forthwith* immediately   105 *by my halidom* bless my soul (originally an
oath by a sacred relic)   110 *Swinge me them* whip them for me

Away, I say, and bring them hither straight.

[Exit Kate.]

LUCENTIO
Here is a wonder, if you talk of a wonder.

HORTENSIO
And so it is. I wonder what it bodes.

PETRUCHIO
Marry, peace it bodes, and love, and quiet life,

115 An awful rule and right supremacy,

116 And, to be short, what not that's sweet and happy.

BAPTISTA
Now fair befall thee, good Petruchio.
The wager thou hast won, and I will add
Unto their losses twenty thousand crowns,

120 Another dowry to another daughter,
For she is changed as she had never been.

PETRUCHIO
Nay, I will win my wager better yet
And show more sign of her obedience,
Her new-built virtue and obedience.

Enter Kate, Bianca, and Widow.

See where she comes and brings your froward wives
As prisoners to her womanly persuasion.
Katherine, that cap of yours becomes you not.
Off with the bauble, throw it under foot.

[She obeys.]

WIDOW
Lord, let me never have a cause to sigh

130 Till I be brought to such a silly pass.

BIANCA
Fie, what a foolish duty call you this?

LUCENTIO
I would your duty were as foolish too.
The wisdom of your duty, fair Bianca,

---

115 *awful* awe-inspiring; *right* proper   116 *what not* everything   130 *pass* predicament

Hath cost me a hundred crowns since suppertime.

BIANCA

The more fool you for laying on my duty.   135

PETRUCHIO

Katherine, I charge thee, tell these headstrong women
What duty they do owe their lords and husbands.

WIDOW

Come, come, you're mocking; we will have no telling.

PETRUCHIO

Come on, I say, and first begin with her.

WIDOW

She shall not.   *140*

PETRUCHIO

I say she shall – and first begin with her.

KATE

Fie, fie, unknit that threat'ning unkind brow   142
And dart not scornful glances from those eyes
To wound thy lord, thy king, thy governor.   144
It blots thy beauty as frosts do bite the meads,
Confounds thy fame as whirlwinds shake fair buds,   146
And in no sense is meet or amiable.
A woman moved is like a fountain troubled,   148
Muddy, ill-seeming, thick, bereft of beauty,
And while it is so, none so dry or thirsty   *150*
Will deign to sip or touch one drop of it.
Thy husband is thy lord, thy life, thy keeper,
Thy head, thy sovereign; one that cares for thee   153
And for thy maintenance; commits his body
To painful labor both by sea and land,
To watch the night in storms, the day in cold,
Whilst thou liest warm at home, secure and safe;
And craves no other tribute at thy hands
But love, fair looks, and true obedience –

---

135 *laying* betting   142 *unkind* (1) unfriendly, (2) unnatural   144 *governor*
ruler   146 *Confounds thy fame* spoils your good name   148 *moved* angry
153 *head* (1) ruler, (2) principle of reason

160 Too little payment for so great a debt.

161 Such duty as the subject owes the prince,
Even such a woman oweth to her husband;

163 And when she is froward, peevish, sullen, sour,
And not obedient to his honest will,
What is she but a foul contending rebel
And graceless traitor to her loving lord?

167 I am ashamed that women are so simple
To offer war where they should kneel for peace,
Or seek for rule, supremacy, and sway,

170 When they are bound to serve, love, and obey.
Why are our bodies soft and weak and smooth,

172 Unapt to toil and trouble in the world,

173 But that our soft conditions and our hearts
Should well agree with our external parts?

175 Come, come, you froward and unable worms,

176 My mind hath been as big as one of yours,
My heart as great, my reason haply more,

178 To bandy word for word and frown for frown.
But now I see our lances are but straws,

180 Our strength as weak, our weakness past compare,
That seeming to be most which we indeed least are.

182 Then vail your stomachs, for it is no boot,
And place your hands below your husband's foot,
In token of which duty, if he please,

185 My hand is ready, may it do him ease.

PETRUCHIO
Why, there's a wench! Come on and kiss me, Kate!

LUCENTIO
Well, go thy ways, old lad, for thou shalt ha't.

VINCENTIO

188 'Tis a good hearing when children are toward.

---

161 *prince* monarch   163 *peevish* obstinate   167 *simple* foolish   172 *Unapt to* unsuited for   173 *conditions* qualities   175 *unable* feeble   176 *big* haughty   178 *bandy* exchange (as in hitting a tennis ball back and forth)   182 *vail your stomachs* curb your willfulness; *no boot* no use   185 *may it* if it may   188 *a good hearing* i.e., good news; *toward* docile

LUCENTIO
  But a harsh hearing when women are froward.

PETRUCHIO
  Come, Kate, we'll to bed.   *190*
  We three are married, but you two are sped.   191
    [To Lucentio]
  'Twas I won the wager, though you hit the white,   192
  And being a winner, God give you good night.
                          Exit Petruchio [with Kate].

HORTENSIO
  Now, go thy ways, thou hast tamed a curst shrew.   194

LUCENTIO
  'Tis a wonder, by your leave, she will be tamed so.
                                              [Exeunt.]

---

191 *sped* done for (through having disobedient wives)   **192** *white* bull's-eye
(playing on "Bianca," white)   **194, 195** *shrew, so* (a rhyme)

The distinguished Pelican Shakespeare series, newly revised to be the premier choice for students, professors, and general readers well into the 21st century

All's Well That Ends Well
ISBN 0-14-071460-X

Antony and Cleopatra
ISBN 0-14-071452-9

As You Like It
ISBN 0-14-071471-5

The Comedy of Errors
ISBN 0-14-071474-X

Coriolanus
ISBN 0-14-071473-1

Cymbeline
ISBN 0-14-071472-3

Hamlet
ISBN 0-14-071454-5

Henry IV, Part I
ISBN 0-14-071456-1

Henry IV, Part 2
ISBN 0-14-071457-X

Henry V
ISBN 0-14-071458-8

Henry VI, Part 1
ISBN 0-14-071465-0

Henry VI, Part 2
ISBN 0-14-071466-9

Henry VI, Part 3
ISBN 0-14-071467-7

Henry VIII
ISBN 0-14-071475-8

Julius Caesar
ISBN 0-14-071468-5

King John
ISBN 0-14-071459-6

King Lear
ISBN 0-14-071476-6

King Lear
(The Quarto and Folio Texts)
ISBN 0-14-071490-1

Love's Labor's Lost
ISBN 0-14-071477-4

Macbeth
ISBN 0-14-071478-2

FOR THE BEST IN PAPERBACKS, LOOK FOR THE 🐧

Measure for Measure
ISBN 0-14-071479-0

The Merchant of Venice
ISBN 0-14-071462-6

The Merry Wives of Windsor
ISBN 0-14-071464-2

A Midsummer Night's Dream
ISBN 0-14-071455-3

Much Ado About Nothing
ISBN 0-14-071480-4

The Narrative Poems
ISBN 0-14-071481-2

Othello
ISBN 0-14-071463-4

Pericles
ISBN 0-14-071469-3

Richard II
ISBN 0-14-071482-0

Richard III
ISBN 0-14-071483-9

Romeo and Juliet
ISBN 0-14-071484-7

The Sonnets
ISBN 0-14-071453-7

The Taming of the Shrew
ISBN 0-14-071451-0

The Tempest
ISBN 0-14-071485-5

Timon of Athens
ISBN 0-14-071487-1

Titus Andronicus
ISBN 0-14-071491-X

Troilus and Cressida
ISBN 0-14-071486-3

Twelfth Night
ISBN 0-14-071489-8

The Two Gentlemen of Verona
ISBN 0-14-071461-8

The Winter's Tale
ISBN 0-14-071488-X

FOR THE BEST IN PAPERBACKS, LOOK FOR THE Ⓟ

In every corner of the world, on every subject under the sun, Penguin represents quality and variety—the very best in publishing today.

For complete information about books available from Penguin—including Penguin Classics, Penguin Compass, and Puffins—and how to order them, write to us at the appropriate address below. Please note that for copyright reasons the selection of books varies from country to country.

In the United States: Please write to *Penguin Group (USA), P.O. Box 12289 Dept. B, Newark, New Jersey 07101-5289* or call 1-800-788-6262.

In the United Kingdom: Please write to *Dept. EP, Penguin Books Ltd, Bath Road, Harmondsworth, West Drayton, Middlesex UB7 0DA.*

In Canada: Please write to *Penguin Books Canada Ltd, 90 Eglinton Avenue East, Suite 700, Toronto, Ontario M4P 2Y3.*

In Australia: Please write to *Penguin Books Australia Ltd, P.O. Box 257, Ringwood, Victoria 3134.*

In New Zealand: Please write to *Penguin Books (NZ) Ltd, Private Bag 102902, North Shore Mail Centre, Auckland 10.*

In India: Please write to *Penguin Books India Pvt Ltd, 11 Panchsheel Shopping Centre, Panchsheel Park, New Delhi 110 017.*

In the Netherlands: Please write to *Penguin Books Netherlands bv, Postbus 3507, NL-1001 AH Amsterdam.*

In Germany: Please write to *Penguin Books Deutschland GmbH, Metzlerstrasse 26, 60594 Frankfurt am Main.*

In Spain: Please write to *Penguin Books S. A., Bravo Murillo 19, 1° B, 28015 Madrid.*

In Italy: Please write to *Penguin Italia s.r.l., Via Benedetto Croce 2, 20094 Corsico, Milano.*

In France: Please write to *Penguin France, Le Carré Wilson, 62 rue Benjamin Baillaud, 31500 Toulouse.*

In Japan: Please write to *Penguin Books Japan Ltd, Kaneko Building, 2-3-25 Koraku, Bunkyo-Ku, Tokyo 112.*

In South Africa: Please write to *Penguin Books South Africa (Pty) Ltd, Private Bag X14, Parkview, 2122 Johannesburg.*